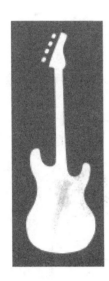

A Rock Reader

Compiled and Edited by

Richard G. King

University of Maryland

KENDALL/HUNT PUBLISHING COMPANY
4050 Westmark Drive   Dubuque, Iowa 52002

Contents

▪▪▪

Part VI. Women in Rock   111

Preface

░░

I have been fortunate to teach the history of rock music in large, first- and second-year classes at the University of Maryland for several years now, using one of the standard textbooks on rock. While that book serves a useful purpose—providing basic chronology, naming the most important songs and musicians, and so forth—I soon realized that it does not deal adequately with many of the significant issues associated with this most important cultural product of our time. Moreover, rock textbooks generally do not give the student a sense of the literature, of the great writing that rock has inspired over the years. I soon realized that a supplement, a course reader, could bring that sense to the students, and so I began to collect what I thought were good examples of writing on rock, and to develop questions that I hoped would bring into focus the critical issues raised in those texts.

This reader is intended as a supplement to courses on rock history, although I hope that it will find other uses. The themes discussed in the articles reproduced here may be broadly categorized as follows: musical history and style, the music industry, technology, drugs and rock, censorship and rock, and women in rock. Other themes that surface here include rock lyrics, rock criticism, and the issue of rock as art. The book is ordered by topic rather than chronology. I leave it to the teachers and students who use this text to decide on an appropriate order for the readings.

The questions that follow each essay are intended to develop critical skills, to focus class discussion, to afford students an opportunity to conduct their own research on a given topic, and to give students practice writing. (Hey, researching and writing about rock? It could be worse!) In particular, the questions are designed to encourage students to bring their own well-developed perspectives on popular music to rock studies. The questions are not necessarily all to be answered; the student or instructor can choose which are most appropriate or most stimulating. I also provide, as an appendix, a series of questions that I have found useful for short-essay assignments.

This book does not pretend to be a comprehensive treatment of the most important themes in rock criticism, nor does it provide comprehensive treatment of the themes it does treat. But if it stimulates critical thinking and discussion, and if these essays provide readers some pleasure, then the book will serve its purpose.

Acknowledgments

■ ■

F irst and foremost, I gratefully acknowledge the contribution of the teaching assistants who helped me to develop this reader—Elizabeth Crouch-Fitts, Joseph Morgan, and Kristian Twombly—and the many students at the University of Maryland with whom I have discussed popular music and from whom I have learned so much. I also thank Boden Sandstrom, for bringing the articles by Helen Kolawole and Amy Raphael to my attention; and the School of Music of the University of Maryland, for encouraging me to teach a course on the history of rock music.

Part

I

History and Style

Classic Rock

■ ■

Nik Cohn

Though Nik Cohn's Awopbopaloobop *purported to be a straightforward résumé of the first decade of rock & roll, there was always a polemical bent to Cohn's prose. Originally published in 1969, under the title* Pop From the Beginning, *it sought to contrast the Classic Rock of Cochran, Berry and Penniman with the shallow sophistry of what came in its wake.*

Rock'n'roll was very simple music. All that mattered was the noise it made, its drive, its aggression, its newness. All that was taboo was boredom.

The lyrics were mostly non-existent, simple slogans one step away from gibberish. This wasn't just stupidity, simple inability to write anything better. It was the kind of teen code, almost a sign language, that would make rock entirely incomprehensible to adults.

In other words, if you weren't sure about rock, you couldn't cling to its lyrics. You either had to accept its noise at face value or you had to drop out completely.

Under these rules, rock turned up a sudden flood of maniacs, wild men with pianos and guitars who would have been laughing stocks in any earlier generation but who were just right for the fifties. They were energetic, basic, outrageous. They were huge personalities and they used music like a battering ram. Above all, they were loud.

It was a great time—every month would produce someone new, someone wilder than anything that had gone before. Pop was barren territory and everything was simple, every tiny gimmick was some kind of progression. Around 1960, things evened out and much of the excitement died out. Pop had become more sophisticated, more creative, more everything. But the fifties were the time when pop was just pop, when it was really something to switch on the radio and hear what was new right that minute. Things could never be so good and simple again.

For instance, the first record I ever bought was by Little Richard and, at one throw, it taught me everything I ever need to know about pop. The message went: 'Tutti frutti all rootie, tutti frutti all tootie, tutti frutti all rootie, awopbopaloobop alopbamboom!' As a summing up of what rock'n'roll was really about, this was nothing but masterly.

Very likely these early years are the best that pop has yet been through. Anarchy moved in. For thirty years you couldn't possibly make it unless you were white, sleek, nicely spoken and phoney to your toenails—suddenly now you could be black, purple, moronic, delinquent, diseased or almost anything on earth and you could still clean up. Just so long as you were new, just so long as you carried excitement.

Most of the best early rockers came out of the South: Elvis from Mississippi, Little Richard from Georgia, Buddy Holly from Texas, Jerry Lee Lewis from Louisiana, Gene Vincent from Virginia. These were the states where the living had always been meanest, where teenagers had been least catered to, and where, therefore, the rock kickback was now most frantic.

Anyhow, the South was by far the most music-conscious section in America, it always had been. It had huge traditions in R&B, country, trad. and gospel, and its music was in every way more direct, less pretentious than that up north. Mostly, it had a sledgehammer beat and pulled no punches. Down here, rock was an obvious natural.

The only innovation was that the rockers made use of all the sources around them. Up to this time, whites had used country, Negroes had used R&B, and the two had never remotely overlapped. Now everyone incorporated anything they could lay their hands on, and it was this mix-up of black and white musics that gave southern rock its flavour.

Of all the great southern rockers, just about the most splendid was the aforementioned Little Richard Penniman out of Macon, Georgia.

He was born on Christmas Day 1935, one of thirteen children, and had a predictably harsh childhood. At fourteen, he was singing solos with the local gospel choir. At fifteen, he was blues-shouting, dancing and selling herb tonic in a medicine show. From there, he got into a variety of groups, made a sequence of nothing

records, and finally in 1955, when he was twenty, sold a million copies of 'Tutti Frutti'.

He looked beautiful. He wore a baggy suit with elephant trousers, twenty-six inches at the bottoms, and he had his hair back-combed in a monstrous plume-like fountain. Then he had a little toothbrush moustache and a round, totally ecstatic face.

He played piano, and he'd stand knock-kneed at the keyboard, hammering away with two hands as if he wanted to bust the thing apart. At climactic moments, he'd lift one leg and rest it on the keys, banging away with his heel, and his trouser rims would billow like kites.

He'd scream and scream and scream. He had a freak voice, tireless, hysterical, completely indestructible, and he never in his life sang at anything lower than an enraged bull-like roar. On every phrase, he'd embroider with squeals, rasps, siren whoops. His stamina, his drive, were limitless and his songs were mostly total non-songs, nothing but bedrock 12-bars with playroom lyrics, but still he'd put them across as if every last syllable was liquid gold. He sang with desperate belief, real religious fervour: 'Good golly, Miss Molly, you sure like a ball—when you're rockin' and rollin', I can't hear your momma call.'

As a person he was brash, fast, bombastic, a sort of prototype Mohammed Ali ('I'm just the same as ever—loud, electrifying and full of personal magnetism'), and right through the middle fifties he was second only to Elvis. Most of his records sold a million each: 'Long Tall Sally', 'Lucille', 'The Girl Can't Help It', 'Keep A Knockin', 'Baby Face'. They all sounded roughly the same: tuneless, lyricless, pre-Neanderthal. There was a tenor sax solo in the middle somewhere and a constant smashed-up piano and Little Richard himself screaming his head off. Individually, the records didn't mean much. They were small episodes in one unending scream and only made sense when you put them all together.

But in 1957 he suddenly upped and quit. No warning—he just stopped touring, stopped making records, and went off to play piano in a Seventh Day Adventist Church off Times Square.

Apparently, he'd been in a plane and a fire had broken out. Richard got down on his knees and promised that if he was spared, he'd give up the devil's music for ever and devote himself to the gospel instead. 'And God answered my prayers and stopped the fire.'

So he announced that he was giving up, but his entourage thought he was crazy and laughed at him. Then Richard, in a typically flash performance, took his many rings from his fingers and flung them into the sea. Almost $20,000 worth: 'I wish I'd seen the face of the man that caught those fish. A king's ransom, all courtesy of Little Richard.' And he quit on the spot. At least, that's the story he tells, and it might be true. Some of his stories are.

Five years he kept it up, made no records, gave no interviews. But in the early sixties he began to cut gospel records, and from there it was inevitable that he'd go back to rock again. He didn't get any further hits, but he was still a name. Several times he toured Britain, and each time he went down a storm.

The first time I saw him was in 1963, sharing a bill with the Rolling Stones, Bo Diddley and the Everly Brothers, and he cut them all to shreds. He didn't look sane. He screamed and his eyes bulged; the veins jutted in his skull. He came down front and stripped—his jacket, tie, cuff-links, his golden shirt, his huge diamond watch—right down to flesh. Then he hid inside a silk dressing-gown, and all the time he roared and everyone jumped about in the aisles like it was the beginning of rock all over again.

Objectively, he didn't even do much. Anyone else that has a great stage act always has an obvious selling point: James Brown has speed, Johnnie Ray has pain, Elvis has sex. Little Richard had none of that. All he had was energy.

He howled and hammered endlessly. On 'Hound Dog', he dropped down on his knees and grovelled, and still he howled. It was all gospel—'that healing music, makes the blind see, the lame to walk, the dead rise up.' He kept it up so long, so loud, it made your head whirl. Good hard rock; he murdered it and murdered us. When he was through, he smiled sweetly. 'That Little Richard,' he said, 'such a nice boy.'

Chuck Berry was a bard; classic rock's definitive chronicler, interpreter and wise-guy voyeur. He wrote endless Teen Romance lyrics but sang them with vicious, sly cynicism and this is the clash that makes him so funny, so attractive.

His most perfect song was 'You Never Can Tell', an effort that gets a lot of its flavour from the knowledge that it was made soon after Chuck had served a hefty jail sentence for transporting a minor across a state boundary without her parents' consent:

> It was a teenage wedding and the old folks wished 'em well,
> You could see that Pierre did truly love the mademoiselle,
> And now the young monsieur and madame have rung the the chapel bell—
> C'est la vie, say the old folks, it goes to show you never can tell.

A jangle piano rambled away legato in the background and there were great swirling sax riffs and Chuck himself more intoned than sang, sly and smooth as always, the eternal 16-year-old hustler. That was it—the Teendream myth that's right at the heart of all pop and 'You Never Can Tell' expressed it more exactly, more evocatively than any of the other fifty thousand attempts at the same theme.

Of course, this is all very naïve and undeveloped by comparison with what has come since, but then Bogart proved thirty years ago that, in mass media, you don't need to be a monster intellectual to be great. In fact, it's a definite disadvantage if you are. What you do need is style, command, specific image and these are the exact things that Chuck Berry has always been overflowing with.

Basically, what it boils down to is detail. Most pop writers would have written 'You Never Can Tell' as a series of generalities and it would have been nothing. But Chuck was obsessive, he was hooked on cars, rock, ginger ale and he had to drag them all in. That's what makes it—the little touches like the cherry-red Jidney '53 or the coolerator.

Chuck was born in California in 1931, grew up in St Louis and, when he was older, got to be a hairdresser. By nature, he was an operator and he was always going to be successful. The only question was how. So he tried singing, he wrote, he made progress. In 1955, he had his first national smash with 'Maybelline' and from then on he was a natural Mister Big.

As a writer, he was something like poet laureate to the whole rock movement. He charted its habits, hobbies, hang-ups or celebrated its triumphs or mourned its limitations and he missed nothing out. 'School Days' pinned down exactly that school-kid sense of spending one's whole life listening for bells and 'Johnny B. Goode', guitar-slinger, created a genuine new folk hero and 'Roll Over Beethoven' should have been adopted as the universal slogan of rock. But almost best of all was 'Sweet Little Sixteen'. Nothing summed up better the twinned excitement and frustration of the time:

> Sweet little sixteen, she's got the grown-up blues
> Tight dresses and lipstick, she's sportin' high-heeled shoes
> Oh but tomorrow morning she'll have to change her trend
> And be sweet sixteen and back in class again.

Beyond his writing, he played a very fair blues guitar, Chicago-style, and sang in a voice as waved and oily as his hair. On stage, his speciality was the duck walk, which involved bound-ing across the stage on his heels, knees bent, body jackknifed and guitar clamped firmly to his gut. Then he would peep coyly over his shoulders and look like sweet little sixteen herself, all big eyes and fluttering lids. He had a pencil moustache and had the smoothness, the cool of a steamboat gambler. A brown-eyed handsome man, in fact.

Just when things were going so well for him, he made his mistake with the minor and was put away. By the time he got out again, in 1963, rock was finished but the British R&B boom was just getting underway and he was made blues hero number one by the Rolling Stones, who started out playing almost nothing but Chuck Berry songs. Almost as a matter of course, he'd landed on his feet.

He was brought over and made much of but turned out to be hard to deal with. He was arrogant, rude. When he liked to turn it on, he could be most charming but often he couldn't be bothered. First and last, he was amazingly mean.

There's an authenticated story about him that, on his first British tour, he used to study the evening paper nightly and check to see if there had been any fluctuation in rates of exchange. If there was any deviation in his favour, no matter how small, he'd demand payment in cash before he went on. On one night, this supplement came to 2s. 3d.

Article 1. Nik Cohn

1. Who was the audience for the music of Little Richard and Chuck Berry?

2. What are some characteristics shared by Little Richard and Chuck Berry?

3. According to Cohn, what is the most important element in rock?

4. Describe another phase of rock's history that illustrates the contrast between raw energy and musical sophistication.

The Emergence of Art Rock

John Rockwell

There is a morphology, an inherent developmental cycle, to artistic movements. They begin with a rude and innocent vigor, pass into a healthy adulthood and finally decline into an overwrought, feeble old age. Something of this process can be observed in the passage of rock & roll from the three-chord primitivism of the Fifties through the burgeoning vitality and experimentation of the Sixties to the hollow emptiness of much of the so-called progressive, or "art," rock of the Seventies.

The whole notion of art rock triggers hostility from those who define rock in terms of the early-middle stages of its development. Rock was born as a street rebellion against pretensions and hypocrisy—of Fifties society, Fifties Tin Pan Alley pop and high art in general ("Roll Over Beethoven"). Thus the very idea of art rock strikes some as a cancer to be battled without quarter, and the punk reversion to primitivism was in part a rejection of the fancier forms of progressive rock. The trouble is, once consciousness has intruded itself into the process, it's impossible to obliterate it (except maybe with drugs, and then only temporarily). And so even primitivism, self-consciously assumed, became one of the principal vehicles of art rock.

The Beatles' *Sgt. Pepper's Lonely Hearts Club Band* (1967) is often cited as the progenitor of self-conscious experimentation in rock. It was the album that dramatized rock's claim to artistic seriousness to an adult world that had previously dismissed the whole genre as blathering teen entertainment. The Beatles aspired to something really daring and new—an unabashedly eclectic, musically clever (harmonies, rhythms and, above all, arrangements) melange that could only have been created in the modern recording studio.

One inevitable implication of the whole notion of art rock, anticipated by *Sgt. Pepper*, is that it parallels, imitates or is inspired by other forms of "higher," more "serious" music. On the whole, imitative art rock has tended to emulate classical music, primarily the eighteenth- and nineteenth-century orchestral sorts. The pioneers in this enterprise were the Moody Blues, whose album *Days of Future Past* paired the group with the London Festival Orchestra. Although Moody Blues devotees seemed to think they were getting something higher toned than mere rock, they were kidding themselves: Moody Blues records were mood music, pure and regrettably not so simple. There's nothing wrong with that, of course, except for the miscategorization into something more profound.

The vast majority of the bands that pillage traditional classical music come from Britain. Why British bands feel compelled to quote the classics, however tongue-in-cheek, leads into the murky waters of class and nation analysis. In comparison with the British, Americans tend to be happy cavepeople. Most American rockers wouldn't know a Beethoven symphony if they were run down by one in the middle of a freeway. One result of such ignorance is that American art (music, painting, poetry, films, etc.) can develop untroubled by lame affectations of a cultured sensibility. In Britain the lower classes enjoy no such isolation. The class divisions and the crushing weight of high culture flourish essentially untrammeled. Rockers seem far more eager to "dignify" their work, to make it acceptable for upper-class approbation, by freighting it with trappings of classical music. Or, conversely, they are far more intent upon making classical music accessible to their audiences by bastardizing it in the rock context. Or, maybe, they feel the need to parody it to the point of ludicrousness. In all cases, they relate to it with a persistence and intensity that American groups rarely match.

The principal examples here from the Seventies are acts like the Nice; Emerson, Lake and Palmer; Deep Purple; Procol Harum; Renaissance; Yes; and Rick Wakeman. Much of what these artists did was just souped-up, oversynthesized, vaguely "progressive" rock of no particular interest or pretensions. But at one time or another all of them dealt in some form of classical pastiche. Wakeman, classically trained as a pianist at the Royal Academy, is as good an example as any. After serving time as a session pianist for the likes of David Bowie and Cat Stevens, he joined Yes, helping to lead the group into a convoluted pop mysticism. He eventually left Yes in 1974 to pursue a solo career devoted to such elaborate, portentously titled orchestral narratives as *Journey to the Centre of the Earth* and *The Myths and Legends of*

King Arthur and the Knights of the Round Table. These ice-skating epics had their elements of elephantine humor. But his classical excursions were dispatched with such a brutal cynicism as to be genuinely appalling.

Even when such groups weren't busily ripping off Grieg their music was operatically arty in the bad sense, through their ponderous appeal to a middle-class sensibility and their lame reliance on electronically updated nineteenth-century vaudeville stage tricks. Too often these pastiches were further burdened by the seemingly irresistible weakness certain sorts of loud, arty British bands had for science-fiction art and "poetry." Yes's album covers make the point as well as anything, but such puerile mythologizing—Tolkien for the teenyboppers—pervaded much of British pop poetry and lapsed over with insufferable affectation into much of the British electric folk-rock camp, too; think only of Jethro Tull and Cat Stevens.

Classical borrowings don't have to be limited simply to quotations, however, nor do they have to be bad by definition. The whole craze for "rock operas" of the Kinks-Who variety produced some fascinating work. Similarly, some of the fairly straightforward heavy-metal groups have colored their music with the judicious application of nonrock styles, to telling effect (the use of Eastern modes and instrumental accents in Led Zeppelin's "Kashmir," for example).

Such use of classical and other nonrock styles and formal ideas blends imperceptibly into all-purpose stylistic eclecticism—the free and often febrile switching among different styles within the same piece. Eclecticism, by now a talisman of the entire post-Modernist movement in all the arts, was more prominent in the Seventies pop world in London than anywhere else, and, at its best, it stops being lamely imitative and enters the realm of creativity.

Numerous British bands of the Seventies fell into the eclectic art-rock camp: Genesis, King Crimson, Electric Light Orchestra, Queen, Supertramp, Sparks, 10cc, Gentle Giant and Be-Bop Deluxe. There were Continental bands like Focus, and even American groups like Kansas, Styx and Boston that fit here also. Certainly there were differences between these groups, large differences, and there were many more groups that could be listed. But they all shared a commitment to unprepared, abrupt transitions from one mood to another. Sometimes the shifts were between tempos, sometimes between levels of volume, sometimes between whole styles of music. The effect in any case was violent, disruptive and nervously tense, and as such no doubt answered the needs of the age as well as anything. At their best (or at their most commercially successful), these groups never lost sight of older rock basics, as with Queen's best work.

In a sense, Roxy Music might be considered the leader of this particular pack, especially between 1971 and 1973, when Brian Eno was a member of the band. But even from the first, and despite the strong contributions of Phil Manzanera and Andy MacKay, this was always Bryan Ferry's band, as proven by the continuity in his subsequent solo albums. Ferry's artsiness expressed itself so much as style over substance that style itself became substantive. As the ultimate self-professed lounge lizard, he managed to take pop-rock's hoariest conventions (the love song, even actual oldies on his solo albums) and coat them with witty intimations of unspeakable decadence. But the real art rocker in Roxy Music was Eno. Aside from the quality of his music, which is considerable and which he sustained into the Nineties, he is interesting from two points of view: his command of the synthesizer and his relation to others on the London and New York experimental scenes.

The synthesizer is a much-abused, much-misunderstood instrument. When played like a souped-up electric organ by people like Keith Emerson, Jon Lord (of Deep Purple) or Rick Wakeman, it can sound simply flashy and cheap. If the obligatory drum solo used to be the bane of any self-respecting rock concertgoer's life, the obligatory synthesizer solo, preferably with smoke bomb and laser obbligato, was the curse of the Seventies. If synthesizers weren't regarded as newfangled organs, they were taken literally, as something that "synthesizes," and we were subjected to Wendy Carlos's and Isao Tomita's synthesized versions of the classics.

The synthesizer is an instrument with its own characteristics, and those characteristics are just beginning to be explored by rock musicians. When played with the subtlety and discretion of a Stevie Wonder or a Garth Hudson, it can reinforce conventional textures superbly. And when somebody like Eno or Edgar Froese of Tangerine Dream gets hold of it, the synthesizer can create a whole world of its own. Eno's *Discreet Music* (1975), with its title-track first side full of soothing, hypnotic woodwindish sounds, or *No Pussyfooting* (1975) and *Evening Star* (1976), two collaborations with Robert Fripp, ex-King Crimson guitarist, or *Music for Airports* (1978), were masterly examples of genuine rock avant-gardism. Of course, they weren't really "rock" in any but the loosest sense: There was no reference back to a blues base, even in attenuated form. But they still counted as music produced by a rock sensibility aimed at a rock audience.

Eno's position within the London avant-garde, and the nature of that avant-garde, are both of interest, too. London, like New York, has a thriving avant-garde musical community that doesn't place much of a premium on formally acquired technique, thus remaining open to fresh infusions of energy from ostensible "amateurs." In London the experimentation in rock was fostered by British taxation, which forced most of the successful commercial rockers out of the country, leaving the rest to experiment relatively free from Top Forty pressures. This robbed the London scene of some potential big-name experimenters like George Harrison (see *Electronic Sound*, 1969) and John Lennon (whose *Two Virgins* with Yoko Ono was another particularly appealing early art-rock entry in 1969).

Still, what was left in the forefront of experimentation was interesting enough. The mere fact that Eno had to leave Roxy Music (quite apart from the question of clashing egos with Ferry) indicates the difficulty of pursuing experimentation and commercial success at the same time. The London avant-garde scene, insofar as any outsider can tell, is marked still by a fascinating if rather private and sporadic interchange between the classical and pop worlds. In the Seventies the pop stars (Eno, guitarist Phil Manzanera of Roxy, Fripp) did rather more interesting work than those who wandered over from a classical background (David Bedford, Stomu Yamash'ta, the Japanese percussionist-turned-rocker). Michael Oldfield fits here to a certain extent, although his work—particularly after his best-selling *Tubular Bells* (1973), which did admittedly have a bland appeal as a reduction of California composer Terry Riley's ideas—was lame beyond recall.

Much of this work, from Oldfield to Eno and even Riley, is head music, and relates to a rather interesting form of avant-garde trance music, which brings us to the subject of drugs. The avant-gardism in rock of the Sixties and Seventies, for all its ultimate debts to surrealism and other vanguard movements from earlier in the century, owed its primary fealty to the proliferation of drugs in the Sixties. It would be misleading to overstress this, but just as false to repress it. Marijuana, LSD and other psychedelics, and methedrine, or speed, all had a profound effect on how music in general, and art rock in particular, was made and perceived. This is not to say that you had to be stoned to play or enjoy this music. But it does mean that the climate and stylistic preoccupations of many varieties of present-day art are built in part on perceptions analogous to the drug experience. Sometimes it takes only one trip, as with acid, to give you a whole other fix on the world.

The kind of quiescent, dappled textural shiftings that mark much of American composer La Monte Young's music (Eno was strongly influenced by Young; and John Cale, formerly of the Velvet Underground, worked closely with him) owe something to grass, at least originally: Maybe Young has never smoked in his life, but his art could have germinated only in a subculture primed for it by marijuana. And the same is true for the whole acid-rock phenomenon.

The pure acid-rockers of the Sixties—from the Byrds to the Jefferson Airplane—don't really concern us here. But Pink Floyd, originally Britain's premier acid-rockers, do. After cutting a couple of British hit singles in 1967, the group concentrated on extended compositions, often with spacey lyrical motifs. *The Dark Side of the Moon* (1973) became one of the most success-

ful albums of the decade, a best-seller in Europe and America as well as England. Floyd turned out some of the most consistently interesting "head music" of the late Sixties and Seventies, and managed, in its various shards after its breakup, at least to re-create some of that work arrestingly thereafter. The group had a sense for line and continuity and ritualistic repetition that was quite special, and to dismiss it simply as technically limited is philistine.

In Los Angeles the drug scene helped spawn the Mothers of Invention, one of the first rock groups to emphasize mixed-media presentations, dubbed "freak-outs" by leader Frank Zappa. Zappa, a self-professed teetotaler, was forced after the first few L.A. freakouts in 1967 to disavow the use of drugs at these affairs—naturally to no avail. The Mothers combined social satire, parody of rock & roll oldies, classical references—Zappa regularly paid homage to Edgard Varèse—and a growing taste for vaguely avant-garde jazz improvisation. It has been an influential collage of styles, affecting the work of such diverse musicians as Jean-Luc Ponty, the jazz violinist, and Paul McCartney, who once cited the Mothers' first album, *Freak Out*, as a key inspiration for *Sgt. Pepper*.

The psychedelic enthusiasms of the late Sixties, kindled by (among others) Pink Floyd and the Mothers of Invention and centered in San Francisco and in London, found their most sustained resonance in the Seventies in West Germany. Kraftwerk had the biggest commercial impact in the United States, thanks to the surprising success in 1975 of *Autobahn*. Rather more interesting was Tangerine Dream and its leader, Edgar Froese. The group's records and Froese's solo albums were impressionistic extravaganzas, full of gentle washes of electronic color. There is a parallel to Eno's work here. But Eno is a more diverse artist than Froese, and more overtly rock oriented, and in such purely experimental pieces as *Discreet Music* he shows an indebtedness to the structuralist principles of classical composers like Young, Riley (himself an offshoot of the psychedelic/meditative climate of the Bay Area in the Sixties), Steve Reich and Philip Glass. Froese, on the other hand, owes his classical inspirations to such orchestral colorists as Hungarian composer György Ligeti and the electronic music of Karlheinz Stockhausen and Iannis Xenakis. Froese's work seems less interesting than that of his models, but at least his choice of inspirations betrayed a certain sophistication.

More directly related to Eno was the band Cluster, with which Eno twice collaborated. And the artier implications of Giorgio Moroder's disco "factory" cannot be ignored here. His "I Feel Love" for Donna Summer is one of the best trance records of the Seventies, among other things—as a version performed in New York by Blondie and Fripp reaffirmed so well. And before he hit upon his disco formula, Moroder had made an overt art-rock synthesizer collage disc, influenced by the German psychedelic groups but better than his models. At the time nobody could be interested in releasing it, and since then Moroder has been too busy to bother.

The evolution of the New York art-rock scene in the late Seventies, and its subsequent spread to Los Angeles and other byways of the United States, was such an eruption of energies that it merits separate treatment. But the pattern suggested by London was brought to triumphant fruition in this country: a rejection of overcomplexity, the development of a new artistic primitivism and finally a direct merger with other forms of avant-gardism, both classical and jazz—with Eno and Fripp, both of whom moved to New York, as catalysts.

This disquisition began with talk about morphologies and self-consciousness, and in some ways the aesthetic behind the New York art-rock scene of the past decade brings us full circle.

Looking at rock from a populist standpoint, one can seriously question both its aspirations to high art and the very hegemony of high art itself. Maybe the self-conscious primitives are right: Maybe art rock doesn't have to be clever complexity at all. Maybe real art is that which most clearly and directly answers the needs of its audiences. Which, in turn, means that we can prize pure rock and pure pop, from Chuck Berry on, as "art" in no way inferior to that which may entail a more highly formalized technique for its execution. Rock may be part of a far larger process in which art broadens its gestures to encompass an audience made more numerous by the permeation of social equality down into strata heretofore ignored.

There is another, more philosophical side to it. What Warhol and pop artists were trying to tell us—and what composer John Cage has been telling us all along—is that art isn't necessarily a product crafted painstakingly by some mysterious, removed artist-deity, but is whatever you, the perceiver, choose to perceive artistically. A Brillo box isn't suddenly art because Warhol put a stacked bunch of them into a museum. But by putting them there he encouraged you to make your every trip to the supermarket an artistic adventure, and in so doing he exalted your life. Everybody's an artist who wants to be, which is really a more radically populist notion than encouraging scholarly studies of the blues. Roll over Beethoven, indeed, and make room for us.

Article 2. John Rockwell

1. How might the metaphor of morphology or life cycle describe the development of rock in the 50s, 60s, and 70s? Can a similar life cycle be seen in rock since 1975?

2. When does the element of seriousness (art) in rock first appear?

3. What kind of music provides the source and inspiration for much art rock music? Why *that* kind of music?

4. Why were most of the art rock groups British, not American?

5. Discuss one musical characteristic common to both eclectic art rock and jazz rock.

6. At what point does art rock cease to be rock? That is, if it has no reference, however distant, to the blues, is it rock?

7. Many define rock in terms of its early (50s) and middle (60s) stages: as rebellion against pretension, against "high art." As John Rockwell has suggested, for them the very idea of art rock is "a cancer to be battled without quarter." Can or should rock aspire to the quality of art, or is raw primitivism its defining quality? You may refer to music or artists from any period of rock's history.

James Brown's Great Expectations

■ ■

Robert Christgau

I'd spent the weekend trying to convince John Rockwell that James Brown was the greatest rock and roller of all time, and my wife was getting bored. This was reasonable—rankings are a boy's kind of thing, very box-score. Still, when I came back and asked her who was the greatest novelist of all time, she saw what I was driving at before she could say Charles Dickens. I wanted her to tell me what she thought a novel should be. Without his mammoth technique— description, character, narrative pull—Dickens wouldn't be in the running. But if that's all there is, one could just as well name Balzac, Austen, Joyce, Dostoyevsky, Faulkner, even Lessing. By choosing Dickens, my wife was pumping more debatable virtues—reach, scope, heart, vulgarity, intuitiveness, yucks. And also, I should add, output—unlike Joyce or Austen, Dickens wrote a lot of books.

With the possible exception of yucks, Dickens' virtues loom large in James Brown's story, too—output and reach most of all. Over the longest peak ever mounted by a rock and roller, from 1960 to 1974, Brown recorded an enormous body of major music, including forty-three singles that made *Billboard*'s top forty. Elvis's career total is over a hundred, but the Beatles and the Stones and Stevie Wonder are also in the forties—as are Michael Jackson if you count his Jackson 5 leads and Diana Ross if you count her Supremes leads (and also, I admit, Elton John, with Pat Boone, Neil Diamond, and the sainted Fats Domino in the high thirties). That's *pop* recognition for an artist who was always better understood by the black audience (well over fifty records in the r&b top ten), *singles* sales for an artist who in 1963 pioneered the LP format in r&b (and the concert-album format in rock and roll) with *"Live" at the Apollo*, an artist who exploded radio's time constrictions like he had disco in mind and left uncharted patches of paradise at thirty-three-and-a third revolutions per minute. Brown cofounded soul and invented funk, and he's powered more good rap records than teen testosterone and Olde English Malt Liquor put together. A singer of epochal grit and grandeur, he did his most daring work as a bandleader whose voice was past its prime. His stance and message were more complex than any rock critic knew, but we who now regard him as the greatest rock and roller of all time are pumping music over meaning—and, meaningfully enough, asserting that in rock and roll the musical component that matters is, you know, rhythm. The song remains the same my goodfoot.

Having plied Rockwell with wild estimates of Brown's ever-burgeoning rep, I felt obliged to poll a cross-section of my colleagues, and at first I was disappointed. Robert Hilburn named Elvis, then John Lennon, then Bob Dylan, with Brown somewhere between four and seven along with Chuck Berry and Jimi Hendrix. Jon Pareles, whom I'd taken for a music man, declared the question unanswerable if not meaningless (as it is), but added that in any case Brown "doesn't have the verbal content" for the top slot. Ever the wag, Greil Marcus unanswered by nominating Jan Berry of Jan & Dean, who he claims did more with less than anybody in the music. But deposed *Boston Phoenix* savant Milo Miles had it Hendrix-Beatles-JB—"definitely number one among living Americans." Dave Marsh, who contributed an evangelistic afterword to the new edition of Brown's 1986 autobiography, responded: "First I'd say it's a mistake to single out just one. Then I'd say James Brown." Nelson George, whose brief reminiscence graces the new *Star Time* box on Polydor, uttered just two words: "James Brown." And Robert Palmer, who mentioned Brown's Georgia mentor Little Richard before demurring from all great-man theories of African-based music, saw my point. Choosing Brown, he suggested, was like choosing Duke Ellington in jazz—honoring a "fundamental structural remaker" rather than an "individual transcendent genius" such as Charlie Parker. "So if you wanted to call him the greatest, I wouldn't argue with that. He pretty much comes closest."

I got my first dose of James Brown theory when Pablo Guzman prodded me into reexamining JB's Polydor output for my seventies book, and even on that mixed evidence—augmented by Cliff White's U.K.-only *Solid Gold* best-of—I was half-convinced. A few years later, Polydor's White-compiled reissues—together with Eric B. & Rakim and "It Takes Two"—completed the job. But for Marsh and George the clincher was the four-CD, five-hour *Star Time*, which inaugurates a new phase of Brownmania. Polydor president Davitt Sigerson, once a damn good critic

himself, projects a series of reissues that will gradually redefine Brown's body of work. Both *"Live" at the Apollo*s will remain, as will the hit-seeking *Roots of a Revolution*, White's dazzling portrait of the young hard worker as r&b polymath, and the patchier *Messing With the Blues*. For chartbound dabblers, a twenty-song best-of is due. Other albums will resurface whole, but Sigerson wants compilations to dominate—some obvious, some obscure, none both at once. He envisions collections of ballads, break-beat rarities, instrumentals from the Pee Wee Ellis and Fred Wesley bands, period overviews that "wash over you like a great African record."

Assuming full corporate follow-through, this is going to be something. Many *Roots of a Revolution* obscurities groove harder than the lesser *"Live" at the Apollo* titles whose studio versions fill out disc one of *Star Time*, and disc four intimates mortality at least twice. But *Star Time* is not only as definitive as these big-bucks boxes are always claiming to be, it's easily the best of them—an astute and generous reinterpretation of an oeuvre that doesn't break down neatly into albums. Its previously unreleased extended takes, which are numerous, never obtrude. And it doesn't come close to exhausting the artist's book. Though a third of it was recorded for King Records between 1965 and 1970—when a black icon infiltrated and then vanished from a pop radio that found "Say It Loud"'s black-and-proud rhetoric easier to take than "Mother Popcorn"'s black-and-complex beats—there's a hell of a lot more where that came from. In 1969 alone, Brown put ten singles on the r&b chart. Seven of them made top ten. Five had the word "Popcorn" in their titles. Only three are on *Star Time*.

I didn't need *Star Time* to convert me. But since Brown's peak was originally over my head and his output beyond my reach, I want to testify that it repays obsessive relistening. Brown's rhythms are arrayed so profusely across the octaves that getting to the bottom of them is irrelevant, and though the pop complaint that his music all sounds the same retains an aura of common sense, it seems ridiculous once you immerse—a way for white people to wish he'd remained the godfather of soul, which they have a handle on, instead of turning his genius to dance music that passeth all understanding. For starters, there's a separate vein of great vocal music. Accurately enough, we think of his voice as a rough, untamable thing—even the pop breakthroughs "Out of Sight" and "I Feel Good" are aggressively staccato. But listen to "Prisoner of Love" and consider what wonders a ballad collection might perform. Cutting a raw power that could give Ray Charles hearing loss is an idiosyncratic yet almost mellow clarity—not the sharp falsetto of a Wilson Pickett, though this unearthly screamer had some of that in him, but a timbre whose expressive resonance verges on normality. The resulting alloy recalls Bobby Bland without sounding like him or anybody else, including funk-period James Brown, and after a dozen or so years of three-hundred-nights-a-year touring it had disappeared from the face of the earth, leaving JB to his true work.

In Cynthia Rose's ambitious book-length critique, *Living in America*, Pee Wee Ellis reports that musicians called "topsy-turvy" bass-and-snare the "New Orleans beat," and that Clyde Stubblefield, who preceded the better-known Jabo Starks into a band they co-chaired for years, "was just the epitome of this funky drumming." This dovetails with Robert Palmer's belief that rather than inventing funk, Brown "codified" the stuttering drums and syncopated bass he'd first encountered fronting Little Richard's New Orleans-bred Upsetters. But I'd put it this way: Brown was the first musician with the vision and guts to put rhythm up top in a pop mix. He did it before soul was a by-word, and even in black music nobody took up the challenge seriously until 1969, when nonpareil funky drummer Ziggy Modeliste led the Meters out of the aforementioned New Orleans. You can hear the beginnings as early as "Out of Sight" in 1964, but it turns out that "Papa's Got a Brand New Bag" was a more literal title than the rhythmically deprived knew. It was also Brown's first top-ten hit, late in the summer of 1965, and nowhere is it described better than in his autobiography: "The song has gospel feel, but it's put together out of jazz licks. And it has a different sound—a snappy, fast-hitting thing from the bass and guitars. You can hear Jimmy Nolen, my guitar player at the time, starting to play scratch guitar, where you squeeze the strings tight and quick against the frets so

the sound is hard and fast without any sustain . . . I had discovered that my strength was not in the horns, it was in the rhythm. I was hearing everything, even the guitars, like they were drums. I had found out how to make it happen."

In an evolution of the ear, Brown's new bag has become the fundament of today's pop—for a decade or more, radio has inundated us with what he put into motion. So the funk titles that fill the three other discs of *Star Time* no longer all sound the same. Just as the songs of the typical popsmith break down into tune families, Brown's break down into groove families, but within the families there's plenty of individual variation—each intro delights the listener with a jolt as hooky as Motown or the Beatles, only it isn't "tunes" that provide the thrill, but riffs. These riffs connect on rhythmic rather than melodic shape (the rock and roll "tune" itself always relied heavily on phrasing), shapes elaborated in patterns perceptible and pleasurable to the mind's ear. Sure they're body music, but you don't need ants in your pants to enjoy them. In fact, often the elaborations are more harmonic than rhythmic. The one slight contradiction in Brown's description of how funk began is that most of the time Brown's jazzy proclivities surface in the horns.

That matters because *Star Time* proves again and again that jazz licks are essential to the unstaunchable freshness of his music. Pee Wee Ellis and Maceo Parker and Dave Matthews are no avant-gardists, but unlike permanent funkateer Fred Wesley, they play jazz on their own, and though by all accounts even these most crucial JB's did exactly what Mr. Brown told them, it was them he told. Avoiding both the solid comfort of Memphis/Muscle Shoals voicings and the busy ornamentation of Brad Shapiro and Dave Crawford's Philly charts, their twisty little furbelows add an acridly urban and perhaps even cosmopolitan wit and bite and backspin to Brown's already intricate beats—check *Star Time*'s nine-minute 1967 "Get It Together," which I'd never heard before, if you think I'm jiving. Texan Cynthia Rose believes Georgian James Brown is a Southerner above all. But the South is a big place and New Orleans is a singular one, and I say that if he hadn't recorded in Cincinnati and lived in New York his Southernness and even his second-line variations would have come out a lot more earthbound, gutbucket, predictable. Brown's soul and funk are deep. But there's also a lightness about him, a transcendent impulse that's built into his concept rather than achieved momentarily in gospelized transport. He's a realist like Dickens, and he's also a formalist like Joyce. Such contradictions always mark the great ones.

Although Rose makes a case for the spellbinding incantation, in-the-moment specificity, and "all-out Southern surrealism" of Brown's "wordplay," and although his mastery of the colloquial is more than sufficient to his needs, "verbal content" is beside the point. So are the political vagaries of a self-made man whose ties to both Hubert Humphrey and Richard Nixon did even more to alienate pop hippies than his black pride. As an African-American conservative prepares to gut the Constitution, there's no reason to take Brown's black self-help philosophy as revealed truth. But it would be blind to deny that it has more currency now than people who couldn't do the popcorn ever dreamed possible, and not just with those who believe in other people's bootstraps. Even as he tells

Dave Marsh that his three-year imprisonment "doesn't have anything to *do* with racism," there's no questioning James Brown's fervid racial commitment, and little doubting that at some organic level that commitment constitutes a species of inaccessibility—an irreducible identity that refuses universalist blandishments and continues to cost him respect.

"I'm not a rock'n'roll singer," says the greatest rock and roller of all time. By this he means not that rock'n'roll has been appropriated by the other man—a phrase he put on record in "Say It Loud—I'm Black and I'm Proud," twenty years before the rappers—but that rock'n'roll is old and he isn't. Even if he was born in 1933 (the books used to say 1928), this is an exaggeration. While no oldies show, his work-release pay-TV special—which began with 1986's "Living in America" and riffed long and loose on an updated version of 1978's "Jam/1980's"—was too iconic by half. But he's made some terrific music since his peak—the last six cuts on *Star Time* represent no serious letdown, and on 1983's *Bring It On* the ballads even sounded good—and it isn't impossible to imagine him doing it again. Some kind of funk-pop cross between *Our Mutual Friend* and *Ulysses* would be nice.

Article 3. Robert Christgau

1. Why does Christgau consider James Brown to be the greatest rock and roller of all time? Do you agree?

2. Some people say that James Brown's music all sounds the same. What does Christgau suggest one has to do to hear it differently?

3. Can this criticism ("It all sounds the same") be applied to other artists?

4. How would you describe Christgau's writing style?

In Which Yet Another Pompous Blowhard Purports to Possess the True Meaning of Punk Rock

■■■

Lester Bangs

If Paul Williams was the founding father of rock journalism then Lester Bangs was the godfather of punk journalism. When 'punk' music was a strictly underground sub-genre, Bangs was espousing the creed in Detroit's very own Creem *of the crop. On this occasion Bangs uses the unorthodox medium of a quickie pop-bio on the rise of Blondie to expound the origins of punk.*

Punk rock was hardly invented by the Ramones in Queens, NY, in 1974–5, any more than it was by the Sex Pistols in London a year or so later. You have to go back to the New York Dolls.

The truth is that punk rock is a phrase that has been around at least since the beginning of the seventies, and what it at common means is rock & roll in its most basic, primitive form. In other words, punk rock has existed throughout the history of rock & roll, they just didn't call it that. In the fifties, when rock & roll was so new it scared the shit out of parents and racists everywhere, the media had a field day. This stuff was derided mercilessly, it was called 'unmusical', it was blamed for juvenile delinquency, sexual depravity (well . . .), if not the demise of Western civilization as a whole. It was said that the musicians could not play their instruments; in large part, by any conventional standards (what they used to call 'good' music), this was true. Does that matter now to the people who are still listening to those classic oldies twenty years later? It was said that the singers could not sing, by any previous 'legitimate' musical standard; this was also true. It was written off nearly everywhere as a load of garbage that would come and go within a year's time, a fad like the hula hoop.

Is any of this beginning to sound vaguely familiar?

The point is that rock & roll, as I see it, is the ultimate populist art form, democracy in action, because it's true: anybody can do it. Learn three chords on a guitar and you've got it. Don't worry whether you can 'sing' or not. Can Neil Young 'sing'? Lou Reed, Bob Dylan? A lot of people can't stand to listen to Van Morrison, one of the finest poets and singers in the history of popular music, because of the sound of his voice. But this is simply a matter of exposure. For performing rock & roll, or punk rock, or call it any damn thing you please, there's only one thing you need: NERVE. Rock & roll is an attitude, and if you've got the attitude you can do it, no matter what anybody says. Believing that is one of the things punk rock is about. Rock is for everybody, it should be so implicitly anti-élitist that the question of whether somebody's qualified to perform it should never even arise.

But it did. In the sixties, of course. And maybe this was one reason why the sixties may not have been so all-fired great as we gave them credit for. Because in the sixties rock & roll began to think of itself as an 'art-form'. Rock & roll is not an 'art-form'; rock & roll is a raw wail from the bottom of the guts. And like I said, whatever anybody ever called it, punk rock has been around from the beginning—it's just rock honed down to its rawest elements, simple playing with a lot of power and vocalists who may not have much range but have so much conviction and passion it makes up for it ten times over. Because PASSION IS WHAT IT'S ALL ABOUT—what all music is about.

In the early sixties there was punk rock: 'Louie, Louie' by the Kingsmen being probably the most prominent example. It was crude, it was rude, anybody could play it, but so what? It'll be around and people everywhere will still be playing it as long as there's rock roll left at all. It's already lasted longer than *Sgt Pepper*! Who in the hell does any songs from that album anymore? Yet, a few years ago, some people were saying *Sgt Pepper* will endure a hundred years.

Seventies punk largely reflects a reaction against the cult of the guitar hero. Technical virtuosity was not a *sine qua non* of rock & roll in the first place and never should have become. Not that brilliant rock hasn't been made by musicians whose technical chops were and are the absolute highest. But see, that's JUST THE POINT. Just because something is simpler than something else does not make it worse. It's just the kind of hype a lot of people started buying in the late sixties with the rise of the superstar and superinstrumentalist concepts.

There was punk rock all through the sixties. The Seeds with 'Pushin' Too Hard'. Count Five 'Psychotic Reaction'. 'Talk Talk' by the Music Machine. And many others. It was simple, primitive, direct, honest music. Then, in 1969, Iggy and the Stooges put out their first album. Throughout the seventies, that and their subsequent two albums became cult items with small groups of people all over the world, who thought these records were some of the greatest stuff they had ever heard. They were also some of the simplest: two chords, a blaring fuzztone, Iggy singing lyrics as simple as 'Can ah cum ovah to-nat? Can ah cum ovah to-nat? Uh said uh we will have a real cool taam—tonaaat! We will hayuv—a reeal coool taam! Tonaat!' Get it? It was, as Ed Ward wrote in *Rolling Stone* when it appeared, 'A reductio ad absurdum of rock & roll that might have been thought up by a mad DAR General in a wet dream.' Except where he was being sarcastic, I thought that was a compliment: the Stooges' music was brutal, mindless, primitive, vicious, base, savage, primal, hate-filled, grungy, violent, terrifying and above all REAL. They meant every note and word of it.

Enter the Dolls. They might have taken some cues from the Stooges, but who they really wanted to be was an American garage band Rolling Stones. And that's exactly what they were. Everything about them was pure outrage. And too live for the time—'72–3–4 mostly. They set New York on fire, but the rest of the country wasn't ready for it.

I was talking to a guitarist friend, and the subject of the Dolls came up.

'God,' she said, 'the first time they were on TV, we just couldn't believe it, that anybody that shitty would be allowed to do that! How did they get away with it?'

I felt like throwing her out of my house. They didn't 'get away' with anything. They did what they could and what they wanted to do and out of the chaos emerged something magnificent, something that was so literally explosive with energy and life and joy and madness that it could not be held down by all your RULES of how this is supposed to be done! Because none of 'em are valid! Rock & roll is about BREAKING the form, not 'working within it'. GIVE US SOME EQUAL TIME. Let the kid behind the wheel. Like Joe Strummer of the Clash says, 'It's not about playin' the chords right, for starters!'

Article 4. Lester Bangs

1. According to Bangs, what is punk rock, and where and when did it begin?

2. What is punk rock today?

3. What are some basic criticisms of punk rock? How are they tied to the musical context from which punk rock arose in the 70s?

4. In what sense is rock & roll democratic?

5. If, as Joe Strummer of the Clash put it, "it's not about playing the chords right, for starters," then what is rock about?

Punk Versus Disco

■ ■

Reebee Garofalo

There are, of course, a number of obvious distinctions between punk and disco. While disco was smooth, sleek, and sensual, punk was dense, discordant, and defiant. While disco depended on technological sophistication and studio production, punk's three chords could be hammered out by any garage band that could get its hands on an electric guitar. While disco dancers aspired to the controlled energy of the gymnast or the precision of group choreography, punks in the "pit" approximated the antics of a tag-team wrestling match. "[P]ogo dancing—jumping up and down and flailing one's arms," observed Charles M. Young, "is as far as one can get from the Hustle." Disco proudly took its place among other black dance music styles. *Rolling Stone*'s Mikal Gilmore suggested that those "rock purists" who dismissed it as "a frivolous form of expression might do well to remember that rock & roll and rhythm & blues were dance styles, too, before they became art forms." Punk, however, had a different agenda. Punk's aim was to deconstruct rock 'n' roll, bleeding it of its black rhythmic influences until only the elements of noise and texture remained. Robert Christgau noted that punk "differentiates itself from its (fundamentally black and rural) sources by taking on the crude, ugly, perhaps brutal facts of the (white and urban) prevailing culture, rather than hiding behind its bland facade." Needless to say, these differences were mirrored in fashion statements that pitted the sheen of polyester leisure suits against the chill of black leather bondage gear and ripped T-shirts held together by safety pins. Fans of each viewed each other with surprise. "It was funny," Legs McNeil, cofounder of *Punk* magazine, has said. "You'd see guys going out to a Punk club, passing black people going into a disco, and they'd be looking at each other, not with disgust, but 'Isn't it weird that they want to go there.'"

Differences as obvious as these tend to obscure the fact that there were certain similarities between the punk and disco cultures. Both were initially shunned by radio (albeit for different reasons) and forced to develop their own countercultural networks. Both were seen as contributing significantly to the destruction of Western civilization—punk with its nihilism, disco with its decadence. Both encouraged active—indeed, fanatical—participation among their

From *Rockin' Out: Popular Music in the USA, 2nd edition* by Garofalo. Reprinted by permission of Pearson Education, Inc., Upper Saddle River, NJ.

audiences. Finally, both arose in reaction to the complacency of the music that preceded them. Compare, for example, Andrew Kopkind on disco with Simon Frith on punk. "Disco in the '70s is in revolt against rock in the '60s," Kopkind explained. "Disco is 'unreal', artificial, and exaggerated. It affirms the fantasies, gossip, frivolity, and fun of an evasive era." Frith, describing the impetus for punk, told his readers that "the reason why teenage music must be *remade* is because all the original rock'n'rollers have become boring old farts, imprisoned by the routines of show biz. . . . I'd rather listen to a good punk rock'n'roll band like the Jam or the Boomtown Rats than to either the old or new work of their original models, the Who and the Stones. But I'm still listening for the old reason—to feel good." The motivation and effect of both genres was quite the same—to intensify the feeling of the moment in an otherwise uncertain world.

Still, most critics at the time decried disco as escapist and embraced punk as a political statement. According to Frith, "The return to rock'n'roll roots is, in itself, a radical rejection of record company habits and punk's musical simplicity is a political statement. The ideology of the garage band is an attack on the star system." Although disco spawned its own multibillion dollar subindustry and punk barely registered a blip in sales, disco made no overt political statement. Herein lies the source of the distortion in the way in which the histories of punk and disco have been recounted. It was punk's political possibilities, real or imagined, that captured the attention of rock critics who had cut their teeth on the political movements of the 1960s. Never has so much been written by so many about so little. As Andrew Kopkind complained in 1979, "John Rockwell was still writing Hegelian analyses of the Sex Pistols in the Sunday *Times* when two-thirds of the city was listening to Donna Summer and couldn't tell Mr. Rotten from Mr. Respighi."

Although disco was seldom intentionally political, in the long run it may have scored a larger political victory than punk. While a good deal of punk, particularly its British variant, was conceived politically, the conflict between its progressive urges and its flirtation with Nazi imagery often led to mixed results in its ability to pull people together. Disco, especially in the United States, brought people together across racial lines not to mention lines of class and sexual preference. It was disco that, as critic Abe Peck has noted, enabled "black artists [to] conquer the pop charts in a way they never did even during the height of rhythm and blues." In such a context, antidisco slogans like "Death to Disco" and "Disco Sucks" have to be regarded more as racial (and sexual) epithets than as statements of musical preference and the systematic avoidance of disco by the rock critical establishment can only be construed as racist, as Mikal Gilmore suggested in 1977:

> [W]henever a phenomenon is given blanket dismissal, you can be sure something deeper is at work. And what's going on here is that rock fans, like the proverbial cake, have been left out in the rain. Disco's principal constituents have been gays, blacks, Hispanics . . . Then coincident with *Saturday Night Fever*, disco achieved anthem-like status with urban, working-class youth. So, in effect, disco had done what punk was supposed to accomplish. . . . rock pride was wounded. Somehow, an entire grassroots movement had passed us by: No wonder Clash fans cry, "Disco sucks!"

By the time the decade had ended, disco had swamped the music business, and punk had imploded. While disco would collapse shortly thereafter, punk would be born again as new wave, incorporating such a wide range of influences that they included disco itself.

Article 5. Reebee Garofalo

1. How do punk and disco differ, and in what ways are they similar?

2. How do you explain the difference between the positive critical reception afforded punk, and the negative reception given to disco?

3. What kind of political victory did disco score that the more overtly political genre of punk could not?

4. Why did 70s punk fail commercially?

5. Would you have belonged in the 70s to the punk or the disco crowd? Why?

The Music Industry

Introduction

■■■

Simon Frith

This book began as an academic text in a British series on "communication and society." It was a solid and generally sober work. I was determined to take rock seriously. I had one eye on my sociological colleagues, still ignoring music in their accounts of the mass media, and the other on my fellow rock fans, still making sense of their music with loose political assumptions left over from the 1960s. I armed my book with footnotes and statistics: everything *I* said was properly documented, every assertion "proved." My approach, cautious objectivity, reflected my position—I was an academic sociologist as well as a rock journalist; but it reflected, too, a wider set of British assumptions about rock and its significance.

When I went to college in 1964 I assumed that I'd reached the end of my teenage bopping days, and I didn't even take my records with me. Rock 'n' roll was heard then, by me too, as youth music—and as working-class music at that; it was time now for me to grow up. Three years later, in 1967, I had an Oxford degree, my entrance ticket to bourgeois culture, and I didn't feel particularly eccentric setting out for California under the inspiration of a pop song, Scott McKenzie's "San Francisco." My use of music hadn't changed after all, and even in England, pop's power was now publicly realized. In Berkeley I found a culture in which rock and politics, music and the Movement, pleasure and action were inextricably linked. They have been so for me ever since, and by the time I came back to England again, in 1969, I was sure that rock was the most interesting and most encouraging of the contemporary mass media.

In the heyday of the counterculture and student organization, this was a widely shared (if rarely examined) assumption. In Robert Christgau's mocking words: "Why is rock like the revolution? Because they're both groovy!" But in the 1970s sociologists turned their attention back to traditional academic matters, and the learned tomes on rock that once seemed likely to appear never materialized. The decline of serious interest in rock was particularly obvious in Britain, where the music had never achieved much cultural respectability anyway. Its status had been as a news event, and the arts editors of the quality press, with a sense of relief, soon shuffled the few rock critics off their pages again. Complacency, rather than disillusion, set in: rock was, after all the alarums, only a matter of fleeting academic concern—just another youth culture quirk.

In order to pursue my musical interests I had to lead a double life: on one hand, going through the paces of an academic sociological career—doing respectable research on youth as a social phenomenon; on the other hand, ringing the changes as a semiprofessional rock writer, contributing my obstinate prejudices and enthusiasms to the thousands of words that accompany the release of every new rock record, the discovery of every new rock star.

My two careers were rarely good for each other: rock writing is not considered suitable for inclusion in an academic curriculum vitae; and "sociology" is a term of abuse among rock writers. However, I didn't lose the convictions that linked my two worlds: rock is a crucial cultural practice and sociological analysis is needed to make sense of it. But I couldn't avoid being defensive either. Nagging questions were always at the back of my mind: Is this topic suitable for sociology? Is this approach right for rock?

My belief in the social importance of rock was sustained by the sales statistics. By the mid-1970s well over $4 billion was being spent annually in the world on musical products, and in America music had become the most popular form of entertainment—the sales of records and tapes easily outgrossed the returns on movies or sports. The British record industry had tripled its output between 1955 and 1975; the collapse of Decca and EMI in 1979 was less a reflection of declining sales than of managerial inability to deal with any situation that wasn't actually a boom. It took the recession to bring home to people how big a business music had become. The difficulties the record industry faces in the 1980s are difficulties derived from success.

The question is: What do such sales figures mean? Sociologists couldn't ignore the record players, tape recorders, and transistor radios found in just about every household by the 1960s, and so records became included in textbook lists of mass media. But this is usually the only mention that records get. Media analy-ses on both sides of the Atlantic continue to be dominated by terms and problems derived from studies of television and the press; records cannot easily be fitted into the subsequent arguments. The figures I've cited are certainly those of a profitable industry, but they don't directly establish records as a mass *medium*. To determine the social power of rock I had to go beyond the account books and sales returns. I had to work my way through definitions of mass communication.

Some aspects of the argument were straightforward. Records are the result of complex organizations. While in live musical experiences the musicians and their audiences are joined by the immediacy of sound, in recorded music they are linked by an elaborate industry. Between the original music and the eventual listener are the technological processes of transferring sound to tape and disc and the economic processes of packaging and marketing the final product; like the other mass media, records rely on capital investment, specialized technical equipment, and on the organization of a variety of skilled roles. The basis of any sociological analysis of records must be an analysis of the record industry, and this will be my focus in Part Two. But the immediate question about record production is this: Are records directed at a large audience? In light of the sales statistics, this may seem a silly question; but it is, in fact, crucial to an understanding of rock as *mass* culture.

"Large" is a relative term in media studies. Mass media have large audiences relative to other media and relative to the number of communicators involved; there is not a given size of audience to which a communication must be addressed to reach mass status. But the position is especially complicated in the case of records because of the relationship between the record industry as a whole and its products, individual records. The record industry is geared to capital accumulation, and its profits depend on the number of records sold. Initial recording costs are once-only expenditures, unaffected by the number of records eventually produced, while the costs of manufacture and distribution are proportionately reduced as the number of records involved increases. The record business is ruled by the logic of mass production, and a large market is its overriding aim.

This market is, however, made up of different audiences buying different records and listening to different musics. And the sales of a particular record can be anything from the handful for an avant-garde recital to the millions for the latest platinum smash from Fleetwood Mac. Should we assume that all records, whatever their genre or sales, are directed at a large audience? Or should we assign some (random?) sales figure that a record must reach before it can be classified as mass communication?

Both approaches are wrong. We can, more constructively, make a distinction between music conceived with no reference to a mass market and music that is inseparable from the mass market in its conception. The former category includes classical music, folk music, and most jazz; the latter category is pop music. Pop music is created with the record industry's pursuit of a large audience in mind; other music is not (and, as we will see, one of the contradictions of rock revolves around this distinction). That classical or folk music can be listened to on records is accidental for its form and content; it is only pop music whose essence is that it is communicated by a mass medium. This is true even though some classical records sell tens of thousands of copies and most pop records are bought by nobody. Pop music is created, however successfully, for a large audience and is marketed accordingly by the record industry; pop records get the bulk of the attention of the advertisers, distributors, and retailers. The assumption is that a pop audience can be *constructed* by the record industry itself. The audiences for classical, folk, and the other "special" forms are, by contrast, not only relatively small (classical music accounts for about 10 percent of record sales in the UK), but also believed to be relatively autonomous—their tastes are "given." The music business can service these tastes but it can't manipulate them.

Pop music doesn't actually have to be on record by this definition—Tin Pan Alley was marketing songs for mass consumption long before the recording industry was flourishing. But at least since World War II pop music has meant pop records. To define "pop" as music aimed at a large market is also, these days, to define it as music aimed at record sales.

Once a record has been issued, there is nothing to stop anyone from listening to it except its price or the (increasingly rare) lack of playback equipment. Radio stations can ban a record from the airwaves, but they can't stop people from buying it: the Sex Pistols' "God Save the Queen" topped the British sales charts despite the banning efforts of the BBC, commercial radio, and even the record shops themselves. Record distributors can't control consumer choice as effectively as can, say, film distributors. Pop records, indeed, have a wider public than any other medium because their availability is not limited by considerations of literacy or language. They can and do cross all national and cultural boundaries. Elvis Presley in the 1950s, the Beatles in the 1960s, Abba in the 1970s were mass media phenomena in nearly every country in the world, and there is a continuous interplay between English, American, and Continental European pop. If anything, Anglo-American mass music dominates the world more effectively than any other mass medium.

It follows that the record-buying public is heterogeneous, coming from a variety of social conditions. This brings me to the central peculiarity of records as a medium: though pop interest is not exclusive to any country or class, to any particular educational or cultural background, it does seem to be connected specifically to age—there is a special relationship between pop music and youth.

The importance of this youth connection becomes clear when we consider the "simultaneity" of record listening. In general terms, the pop public is dispersed: people may listen to the same records, but they do so independently of each other. In what sense, then, is their listening simultaneous? The importance of this concept for other mass media is obvious. Radio listening and television watching are exactly simultaneous activities, and even reading newspapers and magazines can be judged as approximately simultaneous—most people read Tuesday's paper on that Tuesday. But there are no technological or topical reasons why record listening should be so time-bound. People can listen to their records when they choose, and the value of their records is not obviously limited to a particular date. Records can be used with pleasure over and over again (unlike films or many books) and wear out slowly. There are, nevertheless, good economic reasons why records should be time-bound. The record industry depends on constant consumer turnover and therefore exploits notions of fashion and obsolescence to keep people buying.

British record companies issue about 3,000 singles and 3,000 pop albums every year; the American figures are 7,000 singles and 5,000 albums. While a certain proportion of these are rereleases or repackages of old recordings, the majority are new. A good part of the record business involves persuading consumers to buy a record at the moment of its release, to get bored with it after a few weeks, to discard it for a yet newer release, and so on. Pop records are released with a fanfare of publicity, advertising, plugging, and hype. They are produced specifically for the hit parade, which symbolizes simultaneous listening by listing the records that attracted the most purchasers the previous week. The chart's suggestion of continuous musical sensation and change is reinforced by the music press and pop radio, which, by turning pop music into news, make the dating of records even more precise.

As a result, records have a limited active life (for singles it's 60 to 180 days, depending on success) during which time they can be heard on the radio, on jukeboxes, in discotheques. After that they're considered "out-of-date" and cease to be played; they're deleted, only to be revived as "oldies," their appeal then resting on their precise nostalgic connection with a particular date in the past. Individual consumers, encouraged by market pressures, novelty, and fashion, echo this pattern in their own listening. They will give a record a brief active life by listening to it incessantly before sending it to the bottom of the pile when something new comes along; they will bring it out again later only to revive memories.

Only 7 to 8 percent of a year's record releases are hits of this sort—they appear in the charts, get played on the radio, turn up on jukeboxes; but the vast majority of records sold each year come from the Top 30. Records that aren't hits, in other words, don't sell at all. The pop audience buys and listens to the same few records at the same brief moments. The series of apparently individual decisions about what records to buy thus takes on a collective force—everyone makes the same decision. For pop fans themselves, the resulting musical dating process—each sound linked to a specific time— seems so natural that the conservatism of other musical cultures seems inexplicable to them: How can Ernest Tubb fans enjoy exactly the same country show, decade after decade after decade? But it is the "simultaneity" of pop record buying and listening that needs explaining. Are pop fans simply the victims of a commercial process? What are the cultural effects of the patterns of pop collective behavior?

In Britain it is quite clear that the "collective" part of the pop audience is youth. They buy the chart records, read the chart music papers like *Smash Hits* and *Record Mirror*, listen to the national chart stations Radio 1 and Radio Luxembourg. "Old pop," middle-of-the-road, is produced for a mass market but, by and large, lacks young pop's accoutrements—hit parades and magazines and jukeboxes. It takes the form of "standards" with "timeless" appeal. "Quality" pop is broadcast on Radio 2, Britain's easy-listening station, and is featured on the bills of workingmen's clubs and TV variety shows. It is eternal film-score music and background music and difficult to date. Easy-listening music, by definition, neither reflects the historical moment in which it was made nor carries an active sense of its audience. Its "qualities" are negative or, at best, passive.

The distinctions between chart and easy-listening pop are not clear-cut. Easy-listening stars like Barry Manilow do get onto the hit parade; chart toppers like the Beatles make "standards" like "Yesterday"; musicians move from one type of music and audience to the other. And, of course, the chart audience is not exclusively young, nor is the easy-listening audience exclusively old. Nonetheless, the relationship between chart pop and youth has always been taken for granted, not the least by the record business itself, and this relationship lies at the heart of pop music's cultural importance. In most respects, pop consumers make up just another impersonal and anonymous mass public—the music marketplace is not, in any organized sense, anything more than a collection of individuals. But *young* consumers have a sense of being part of a common audience, whether a generation or a cult. Pop stars since Elvis Presley have been, from whatever distance, a part of this community—they are also young. It is with reference to youth that we have to examine the issues of manipulation and its meaning: the sociology of rock is inseparable from the sociology of youth.

In Britain, certainly, it is easier to justify the sociology of rock in terms of youth culture than in terms of mass culture. Britain's few academic theories of rock have emerged from studies of youth, and this reflects a general cultural point: music is integrated into youth cultures in Britain in ways that it isn't in America (punk is only the most recent example of this use of music as a subcultural sign). The history of British pop audiences has always been a history of British youth styles.

The same point can be made the other way around: America has an adult music audience of a sort unknown in Britain, where, throughout the 1970s, people still stopped buying new records at the age of twenty-five. America has a visible rock generation, weaned on rock 'n' roll and still serviced by new music as it moves into affluence and parenthood. The contrast between audiences is obvious in the music press. America's *Rolling Stone* has grown with its readers, its consumer tips becoming steadily more middle-aged. The British music papers, by contrast, are written for an ever-changing audience of the same teen age. Hence, the contrasting treatments of punk: *Rolling Stone*, detached, grudging, patronizing; *New Musical Express*, half cynically, half joyously, leaping into the maelstrom itself.

For all this, there is obviously a special relationship between music and American youth cultures, too, but the social significance of rock is not *defined* in terms of youth in America as it is in Britain. Rather, youth itself is defined differently, as an ideological and not just an age category. (I'll return to the ques-

tions this raises—about youth and the family, about leisure and pleasure—in Part Three.) The point I want to stress here is that from these different assumptions about the pop audience come different accounts of what popular music means.

American rock writers are mythologists: they comb music for symbolic significance, and their symbols are derived from a sweep through American culture in general. These rock critics write (and are read) as American culture critics. British rock writers, by contrast, are still pop fans, still isolated in a cult world. Their writing is a matter of documentation (the most loving archivists of American popular music are Britons) or solidarity—British writers have an acute sense of their young readers and their needs. And the issue here isn't just a critical strategy; there's also a problem of definition. The sociology of rock is, in the end, determined by its object of study. The ultimate question—one I've been avoiding—is: What is rock?

The implication of the argument I've been making is that rock (as an aspect of pop) can be defined in purely sociological terms, by reference simply to the process of its production and consumption: rock is music produced commercially for simultaneous consumption by a mass youth market. But rock can also be defined in musical terms, as a pop genre (the sound of the early seventies?). And rock is, further, an ideological suffix. To add "rock" to a musical description (folk-rock, country-rock, punk-rock) is to draw attention not just to a sound and a beat but also to an intention and an effect.

Rock, in contrast to pop, carries intimations of sincerity, authenticity, art—noncommercial concerns. These intimations have been muffled since rock became the record industry, but it is the possibilities, the promises, that matter. The trouble with a purely sociological definition of rock is that the object of the definition, the music itself, tends to disappear from view. This is a hazard I've always been aware of as a rock critic: I'm too easily drawn to other tasks—biography, history, commercial accounting, the iconography of youth—when the central task is to account for the pleasure of the musical texts themselves. The sociology of rock must be, in the end, the sociology of musical experiences, and these really can't be defined in terms of their commercial or youthful context. Rather than deducing the meaning of rock from the processes of its production and consumption, we have to try to make sense of rock's production and consumption on the basis of what is at stake in these processes—the meanings that are produced and consumed. Rock is a mass-produced music that carries a critique of its own means of production; it is a mass-consumed music that constructs its own "authentic" audience. The purpose of this book is to explain these contradictions.

A final note: rock is an American music, and much of what I'm going to say will draw on British experience and British examples. I'm not apologetic about this—my rock experience is a British experience, and it is this, ultimately, that I am trying to understand. And there are advantages in my position: rock is both a medium general to capitalist cultures and a specifically American form of music. How American music was generalized, how American sounds—pop and rock—are experienced (and produced) in other cultural contexts are important questions in themselves. The issue here is not just musical meaning, but also the slipperiness, the power, the idea of "America" itself.

Article 6. Simon Frith

1. What is Frith's explanation of why pop tunes age quickly? Does his explanation satisfy you?

2. Dealing with rock as a social phenomenon leaves out one essential element, which is? Why is this element missing from so much rock criticism?

3. Rock crosses all boundaries and borders but one. Which? And why?

4. How does Frith distinguish between rock and pop? How would you define them?

5. What surprised you most about the industry as described by Frith?

Courtney Love Does the Math

●●●

Courtney Love

The controversial singer takes on record label profits, Napster and "sucka VCs."

June 14, 2000 | Today I want to talk about piracy and music. What is piracy? Piracy is the act of stealing an artist's work without any intention of paying for it. I'm not talking about Napster-type software.

I'm talking about major label recording contracts.

I want to start with a story about rock bands and record companies, and do some recording-contract math:

This story is about a bidding-war band that gets a huge deal with a 20 percent royalty rate and a million-dollar advance. (No bidding-war band ever got a 20 percent royalty, but whatever.) This is my "funny" math based on some reality and I just want to qualify it by saying I'm positive it's better math than what Edgar Bronfman Jr. [the president and CEO of Seagram, which owns Polygram] would provide.

What happens to that million dollars?

They spend half a million to record their album. That leaves the band with $500,000. They pay $100,000 to their manager for 20 percent commission. They pay $25,000 each to their lawyer and business manager.

That leaves $350,000 for the four band members to split. After $170,000 in taxes, there's $180,000 left. That comes out to $45,000 per person.

That's $45,000 to live on for a year until the record gets released.

The record is a big hit and sells a million copies. (How a bidding-war band sells a million copies of its debut record is another rant entirely, but it's based on any basic civics-class knowledge that any of us have about cartels. Put simply, the antitrust laws in this country are basically a joke, protecting us just enough to not have to re-name our park service the Phillip Morris National Park Service.)

So, this band releases two singles and makes two videos. The two videos cost a million dollars to make and 50 percent of the video production costs are recouped out of the band's royalties.

The band gets $200,000 in tour support, which is 100 percent recoupable.

The record company spends $300,000 on independent radio promotion. You have to pay independent promotion to get your song on the radio; independent promotion is a system where the record companies use middlemen so they can pretend not to know that radio stations—the unified broadcast system—are getting paid to play their records.

All of those independent promotion costs are charged to the band.

Since the original million-dollar advance is also recoupable, the band owes $2 million to the record company.

If all of the million records are sold at full price with no discounts or record clubs, the band earns $2 million in royalties, since their 20 percent royalty works out to $2 a record.

Two million dollars in royalties minus $2 million in recoupable expenses equals . . . zero!

How much does the record company make?

They grossed $11 million.

It costs $500,000 to manufacture the CDs and they advanced the band $1 million. Plus there were $1 million in video costs, $300,000 in radio promotion and $200,000 in tour support.

The company also paid $750,000 in music publishing royalties.

They spent $2.2 million on marketing. That's mostly retail advertising, but marketing also pays for those huge posters of Marilyn Manson in Times Square and the street scouts who drive around in vans handing out black Korn T-shirts and backwards baseball caps. Not to mention trips to Scores and cash for tips for all and sundry.

Add it up and the record company has spent about $4.4 million.

So their profit is $6.6 million; the band may as well be working at a 7-Eleven.

Of course, they had fun. Hearing yourself on the radio, selling records, getting new fans and being on TV is great, but now the band doesn't have enough money to pay the rent and nobody has any credit.

Worst of all, after all this, the band owns none of its work . . . they can pay the mortgage forever but they'll never own the house. Like I said: Sharecropping. Our media says, "Boo hoo, poor pop stars, they had a nice ride. Fuck them

for speaking up"; but I say this dialogue is imperative. And cynical media people, who are more fascinated with celebrity than most celebrities, need to reacquaint themselves with their value systems.

When you look at the legal line on a CD, it says copyright 1976 Atlantic Records or copyright 1996 RCA Records. When you look at a book, though, it'll say something like copyright 1999 Susan Faludi, or David Foster Wallace. Authors own their books and license them to publishers. When the contract runs out, writers gets their books back. But record companies own our copyrights forever.

The system's set up so almost nobody gets paid.

Recording Industry Association of America (RIAA)

Last November, a Congressional aide named Mitch Glazier, with the support of the RIAA, added a "technical amendment" to a bill that defined recorded music as "works for hire" under the 1978 Copyright Act.

He did this after all the hearings on the bill were over. By the time artists found out about the change, it was too late. The bill was on its way to the White House for the president's signature.

That subtle change in copyright law will add billions of dollars to record company bank accounts over the next few years—billions of dollars that rightfully should have been paid to artists. A "work for hire" is now owned in perpetuity by the record company.

Under the 1978 Copyright Act, artists could reclaim the copyrights on their work after 35 years. If you wrote and recorded "Everybody Hurts," you at least got it back as a family legacy after 35 years. But now, because of this corrupt little pisher, "Everybody Hurts" never gets returned to your family, and can now be sold to the highest bidder.

Over the years record companies have tried to put "work for hire" provisions in their contracts, and Mr. Glazier claims that the "work for hire" only "codified" a standard industry practice. But copyright laws didn't identify sound recordings as being eligible to be called "works for hire," so those contracts didn't mean anything. Until now.

Writing and recording "Hey Jude" is now the same thing as writing an English textbook, writing standardized tests, translating a novel from one language to another or making a map. These are the types of things addressed in the "work for hire" act. And writing a standardized test is a work for hire. Not making a record.

So an assistant substantially altered a major law when he only had the authority to make spelling corrections. That's not what I learned about how government works in my high school civics class.

Three months later, the RIAA hired Mr. Glazier to become its top lobbyist at a salary that was obviously much greater than the one he had as the spelling corrector guy.

The RIAA tries to argue that this change was necessary because of a provision in the bill that musicians supported. That provision prevents anyone from registering a famous person's name as a Web address without that person's permission. That's great. I own my name, and should be able to do what I want with my name.

But the bill also created an exception that allows a company to take a person's name for a Web address if they create a work for hire. Which means a record company would be allowed to own your Web site when you record your "work for hire" album. Like I said: Sharecropping.

Although I've never met any one at a record company who "believed in the Internet," they've all been trying to cover their asses by securing everyone's digital rights. Not that they know what to do with them. Go to a major label-owned band site. Give me a dollar for every time you see an annoying "under construction" sign. I used to pester Geffen (when it was a label) to do a better job. I was totally ignored for two years, until I got my band name back. The Goo Goo Dolls are struggling to gain control of their domain name from Warner Bros., who claim they own the name because they set up a shitty promotional Web site for the band.

Orrin Hatch, songwriter and Republican senator from Utah, seems to be the only person in Washington with a progressive view of copyright law. One lobbyist says that there's no one in the House with a similar view and that "this would have never happened if Sonny Bono was still alive."

By the way, which bill do you think the recording industry used for this amendment?

The Record Company Redefinition Act? No. The Music Copyright Act? No. The Work for Hire Authorship Act? No.

How about the Satellite Home Viewing Act of 1999?

Stealing our copyright reversions in the dead of night while no one was looking, and with no hearings held, is piracy.

It's piracy when the RIAA lobbies to change the bankruptcy law to make it more difficult for musicians to declare bankruptcy. Some musicians have declared bankruptcy to free themselves from truly evil contracts. TLC declared bankruptcy after they received less than 2 percent of the $175 million earned by their CD sales. That was about 40 times less than the profit that was divided among their management, production and record companies.

Toni Braxton also declared bankruptcy in 1998. She sold $188 million worth of CDs, but she was broke because of a terrible recording contract that paid her less than 35 cents per album. Bankruptcy can be an artist's only defense against a truly horrible deal and the RIAA wants to take it away.

Artists want to believe that we can make lots of money if we're successful. But there are hundreds of stories about artists in their 60s and 70s who are broke because they never made a dime from their hit records. And real success is still a long shot for a new artist today. Of the 32,000 new releases each year, only 250 sell more than 10,000 copies. And less than 30 go platinum.

The four major record corporations fund the RIAA. These companies are rich and obviously well-represented. Recording artists and musicians don't really have the money to compete. The 273,000 working musicians in America make about $30,000 a year. Only 15 percent of American Federation of Musicians members work steadily in music.

But the music industry is a $40 billion-a-year business. One-third of that revenue comes from the United States. The annual sales of cassettes, CDs and video are larger than the gross national product of 80 countries. Americans have more CD players, radios and VCRs than we have bathtubs.

Story after story gets told about artists—some of them in their 60s and 70s, some of them authors of huge successful songs that we all enjoy, use and sing—living in total poverty, never having been paid anything. Not even having access to a union or to basic health care. Artists who have generated billions of dollars for an industry die broke and un-cared for.

And they're not actors or participators. They're the rightful owners, originators and performers of original compositions.

This is piracy.

Technology Is Not Piracy

This opinion is one I really haven't formed yet, so as I speak about Napster now, please understand that I'm not totally informed. I will be the first in line to file a class action suit to protect my copyrights if Napster or even the far more advanced Gnutella doesn't work with us to protect us. I'm on [Metallica drummer] Lars Ulrich's side, in other words, and I feel really badly for him that he doesn't know how to condense his case down to a sound-bite that sounds more reasonable than the one I saw today.

I also think Metallica is being given too much grief. It's anti-artist, for one thing. An artist speaks up and the artist gets squashed: Sharecropping. Don't get above your station, kid. It's not piracy when kids swap music over the Internet using Napster or Gnutella or Freenet or iMesh or beaming their CDs into a My.MP3.com or MyPlay.com music locker. It's piracy when those guys that run those companies make side deals with the cartel lawyers and label heads so that they can be "the labels' friend," and not the artists'.

Recording artists have essentially been giving their music away for free under the old system, so new technology that exposes our music to a larger audience can only be a good thing. Why aren't these companies working with us to create some peace?

There were a billion music downloads last year, but music sales are up. Where's the evi-

dence that downloads hurt business? Downloads are creating more demand.

Why aren't record companies embracing this great opportunity? Why aren't they trying to talk to the kids passing compilations around to learn what they like? Why is the RIAA suing the companies that are stimulating this new demand? What's the point of going after people swapping cruddy-sounding MP3s? Cash! Cash they have no intention of passing onto us, the writers of their profits.

At this point the "record collector" geniuses who use Napster don't have the coolest most arcane selection anyway, unless you're into techno. Hardly any pre-1982 REM fans, no '60s punk, even the Alan Parsons Project was underrepresented when I tried to find some Napster buddies. For the most part, it was college boy rawk without a lot of imagination. Maybe that's the demographic that cares—and in that case, My Bloody Valentine and Bert Jansch aren't going to get screwed just yet. There's still time to negotiate.

Destroying Traditional Access

Somewhere along the way, record companies figured out that it's a lot more profitable to control the distribution system than it is to nurture artists. And since the companies didn't have any real competition, artists had no other place to go. Record companies controlled the promotion and marketing; only they had the ability to get lots of radio play, and get records into all the big chain stores. That power put them above both the artists and the audience. They own the plantation.

Being the gatekeeper was the most profitable place to be, but now we're in a world half without gates. The Internet allows artists to communicate directly with their audiences; we don't have to depend solely on an inefficient system where the record company promotes our records to radio, press or retail and then sits back and hopes fans find out about our music.

Record companies don't understand the intimacy between artists and their fans. They put records on the radio and buy some advertising and hope for the best. Digital distribution gives everyone worldwide, instant access to music.

And filters are replacing gatekeepers. In a world where we can get anything we want, whenever we want it, how does a company create value? By filtering. In a world without friction, the only friction people value is editing. A filter is valuable when it understands the needs of both artists and the public. New companies should be conduits between musicians and their fans.

Right now the only way you can get music is by shelling out $17. In a world where music costs a nickel, an artist can "sell" 100 million copies instead of just a million.

The present system keeps artists from finding an audience because it has too many artificial scarcities: limited radio promotion, limited bin space in stores and a limited number of spots on the record company roster.

The digital world has no scarcities. There are countless ways to reach an audience. Radio is no longer the only place to hear a new song. And tiny mall record stores aren't the only place to buy a new CD.

I'm Leaving

Now artists have options. We don't have to work with major labels anymore, because the digital economy is creating new ways to distribute and market music. And the free ones amongst us aren't going to. That means the slave class, which I represent, has to find ways to get out of our deals. This didn't really matter before, and that's why we all stayed.

I want my seven-year contract law California labor code case to mean something to other artists. (Universal Records sues me because I leave because my employment is up, but they say a recording contract is not a personal contract; because the recording industry—who, we have established, are excellent lobbyists, getting, as they did, a clerk to disallow Don Henley or Tom Petty the right to give their copyrights to their families—in California, in 1987, lobbied to pass an amendment that nullified recording contracts as personal contracts, sort of. Maybe. Kind of. A little bit. And again, in the dead of night, succeeded.)

That's why I'm willing to do it with a sword in my teeth. I expect I'll be ignored or ostracized following this lawsuit. I expect that the treatment you're seeing Lars Ulrich get now will

quadruple for me. Cool. At least I'll serve a purpose. I'm an artist and a good artist, I think, but I'm not that artist that has to play all the time, and thus has to get fucked. Maybe my laziness and self-destructive streak will finally pay off and serve a community desperately in need of it. They can't torture me like they could Lucinda Williams.

You Funny Dot-Communists. Get Your Shit Together, You Annoying Sucka VCs

I want to work with people who believe in music and art and passion. And I'm just the tip of the iceberg. I'm leaving the major label system and there are hundreds of artists who are going to follow me. There's an unbelievable opportunity for new companies that dare to get it right.

How can anyone defend the current system when it fails to deliver music to so many potential fans? That only expects of itself a "5 percent success rate" a year? The status quo gives us a boring culture. In a society of over 300 million people, only 30 new artists a year sell a million records. By any measure, that's a huge failure.

Maybe each fan will spend less money, but maybe each artist will have a better chance of making a living. Maybe our culture will get more interesting than the one currently owned by Time Warner. I'm not crazy. Ask yourself, are any of you somehow connected to Time Warner media? I think there are a lot of yeses to that and I'd have to say that in that case president McKinley truly failed to bust any trusts. Maybe we can remedy that now.

Artists will make that compromise if it means we can connect with hundreds of millions of fans instead of the hundreds of thousands that we have now. Especially if we lose all the crap that goes with success under the current system. I'm willing, right now, to leave half of these trappings—fuck it, all these trappings—at the door to have a pure artist experience. They cosset us with trappings to shut us up. That way when we say "sharecropper!" you can point to my free suit and say "Shut up pop star."

Here, take my Prada pants. Fuck it. Let us do our real jobs. And those of us addicted to celebrity because we have nothing else to give will fade away. And those of us addicted to celebrity because it was there will find a better, purer way to live.

Since I've basically been giving my music away for free under the old system, I'm not afraid of wireless, MP3 files or any of the other threats to my copyrights. Anything that makes my music more available to more people is great. MP3 files sound cruddy, but a well-made album sounds great. And I don't care what anyone says about digital recordings. At this point they are good for dance music, but try listening to a warm guitar tone on them. They suck for what I do.

Record companies are terrified of anything that challenges their control of distribution. This is the business that insisted that CDs be sold in incredibly wasteful 6-by-12 inch long boxes just because no one thought you could change the bins in a record store.

Let's not call the major labels "labels." Let's call them by their real names: They are the distributors. They're the only distributors and they exist because of scarcity. Artists pay 95 percent of whatever we make to gatekeepers because we used to need gatekeepers to get our music heard. Because they have a system, and when they decide to spend enough money— all of it recoupable, all of it owed by me—they can occasionally shove things through this system, depending on a lot of arbitrary factors.

The corporate filtering system, which is the system that brought you (in my humble opinion) a piece of crap like "Mambo No. 5" and didn't let you hear the brilliant Cat Power record or the amazing new Sleater Kinney record, obviously doesn't have good taste anyway. But we've never paid major label/distributors for their good taste. They've never been like Yahoo and provided a filter service.

There were a lot of factors that made a distributor decide to push a recording through the system:

How powerful is management?

Who owes whom a favor?

What independent promoter's cousin is the drummer?

What part of the fiscal year is the company putting out the record?

Is the royalty rate for the artist so obscenely bad that it's almost 100 percent profit instead of just 95 percent so that if the record sells, it's literally a steal?

How much bin space is left over this year?

Was the record already a hit in Europe so that there's corporate pressure to make it work?

Will the band screw up its live career to play free shows for radio stations?

Does the artist's song sound enough like someone else that radio stations will play it because it fits the sound of the month?

Did the artist get the song on a film soundtrack so that the movie studio will pay for the video?

These factors affect the decisions that go into the system. Not public taste. All these things are becoming eradicated now. They are gone or on their way out. We don't need the gatekeepers any more. We just don't need them.

And if they aren't going to do for me what I can do for myself with my 19-year-old Webmistress on my own Web site, then they need to get the hell out of my way. [I will] allow millions of people to get my music for nothing if they want and hopefully they'll be kind enough to leave a tip if they like it.

I still need the old stuff. I still need a producer in the creation of a recording, I still need to get on the radio (which costs a lot of money), I still need bin space for hardware CDs, I still need to provide an opportunity for people without computers to buy the hardware that I make. I still need a lot of this stuff, but I can get these things from a joint venture with a company that serves as a conduit and knows its place. Serving the artist and serving the public: That's its place.

Equity for Artists

A new company that gives artists true equity in their work can take over the world, kick ass and make a lot of money. We're inspired by how people get paid in the new economy. Many visual artists and software and hardware designers have real ownership of their work.

I have a 14-year-old niece. She used to want to be a rock star. Before that she wanted to be an actress. As of six months ago, what do you think she wants to be when she grows up? What's the glamorous, emancipating career of choice? Of course, she wants to be a Web designer. Its such a glamorous business!

When you people do business with artists, you have to take a different view of things. We want to be treated with the respect that now goes to Web designers. We're not Dockers-wearing Intel workers from Portland who know how to "manage our stress." We don't understand or want to understand corporate culture.

I feel this obscene gold rush greedgreedgreed vibe that bothers me a lot when I talk to dot-com people about all this. You guys can't hustle artists that well. At least slick A&R guys know the buzzwords. Don't try to compete with them. I just laugh at you when you do! Maybe you could a year ago when anything dot-com sounded smarter than the rest of us, but the scam has been uncovered.

The celebrity-for-sale business is about to crash, I hope, and the idea of a sucker VC gifting some company with four floors just because they can "do" "chats" with "Christina" once or twice is ridiculous. I did a chat today, twice. Big damn deal. 200 bucks for the software and some elbow grease and a good back-end coder. Wow. That's not worth 150 million bucks.

. . . I mean, yeah, sure it is if you'd like to give it to me.

Tipping/Music as Service

I know my place. I'm a waiter. I'm in the service industry.

I live on tips. Occasionally, I'm going to get stiffed, but that's OK. If I work hard and I'm doing good work, I believe that the people who enjoy it are going to want to come directly to me and get my music because it sounds better, since it's mastered and packaged by me personally. I'm providing an honest, real experience. Period.

When people buy the bootleg T-shirt in the concert parking lot and not the more expensive T-shirt inside the venue, it isn't to save money. The T-shirt in the parking lot is cheap and badly made, but it's easier to buy. The bootleggers have a better distribution system. There's no waiting in line and it only takes two minutes to buy one.

I know that if I can provide my own T-shirt that I designed, that I made, and provide it as quickly or quicker than the bootleggers, people who've enjoyed the experience I've provided will be happy to shell out a little more

money to cover my costs. Especially if they understand this context, and aren't being shoveled a load of shit about "uppity" artists.

It's exactly the same with recorded music. The real thing to fear from Napster is its simple and excellent distribution system. No one really prefers a cruddy-sounding Napster MP3 file to the real thing. But it's really easy to get an MP3 file; and in the middle of Kansas you may never see my record because major distribution is really bad if your record's not in the charts this week, and even then it takes a couple of weeks to restock the one copy they usually keep on hand.

I also know how many times I have heard a song on the radio that I loved only to buy the record and have the album be a piece of crap. If you're afraid of your own filler then I bet you're afraid of Napster. I'm afraid of Napster because I think the major label cartel will get to them before I do.

I've made three records. I like them all. I haven't made filler and they're all committed pieces of work. I'm not scared of you previewing my record. If you like it enough to have it be a part of your life, I know you'll come to me to get it, as long as I show you how to get to me, and as long as you know that it's out.

Most people don't go into restaurants and stiff waiters, but record labels represent the restaurant that forces the waiters to live on, and sometimes pool, their tips. And they even fight for a bit of their tips.

Music is a service to its consumers, not a product. I live on tips. Giving music away for free is what artists have been doing naturally all their lives.

New Models

Record companies stand between artists and their fans. We signed terrible deals with them because they controlled our access to the public.

But in a world of total connectivity, record companies lose that control. With unlimited bin space and intelligent search engines, fans will have no trouble finding the music they know they want. They have to know they want it, and that needs to be a marketing business that takes a fee.

If a record company has a reason to exist, it has to bring an artist's music to more fans and it has to deliver more and better music to the audience. You bring me a bigger audience or a better relationship with my audience or get the fuck out of my way. Next time I release a record, I'll be able to go directly to my fans and let them hear it before anyone else.

We'll still have to use radio and traditional CD distribution. Record stores aren't going away any time soon and radio is still the most important part of record promotion.

Major labels are freaking out because they have no control in this new world. Artists can sell CDs directly to fans. We can make direct deals with thousands of other Web sites and promote our music to millions of people that old record companies never touch.

We're about to have lots of new ways to sell our music: downloads, hardware bundles, memory sticks, live Webcasts, and lots of other things that aren't even invented yet.

Content Providers

But there's something you guys have to figure out.

Here's my open letter to Steve Case:

Avatars don't talk back!!! But what are you going to do with real live artists?

Artists aren't like you. We go through a creative process that's demented and crazy. There's a lot of soul-searching and turning ourselves inside-out and all kinds of gross stuff that ends up on "Behind the Music."

A lot of people who haven't been around artists very much get really weird when they sit down to lunch with us. So I want to give you some advice: Learn to speak our language. Talk about songs and melody and hooks and art and beauty and soul. Not sleazy record-guy crap, where you're in a cashmere sweater murmuring that the perfect deal really *is* perfect, Courtney. Yuck. Honestly hire honestly committed people. We're in a "new economy," right? You can afford to do that.

But don't talk to me about "content."

I get really freaked out when I meet someone and they start telling me that I should record 34 songs in the next six months so that we have enough content for my site. Defining

artistic expression as content is anathema to me.

What the hell is content? Nobody buys content. Real people pay money for music because it means something to them. A great song is not just something to take up space on a Web site next to stock market quotes and baseball scores.

DEN tried to build a site with artist-free content and I'm not sorry to see it fail. The DEN shows look like art if you're not paying attention, but they forgot to hire anyone to be creative. So they ended up with a lot of content nobody wants to see because they thought they could avoid dealing with defiant and moody personalities. Because they were arrogant. And because they were conformists. Artists have to deal with business people and business people have to deal with artists. We hate each other. Let's create companies of mediators.

Every single artist who makes records believes and hopes that they give you something that will transform your life. If you're really just interested in data mining or selling banner ads, stick with those "artists" willing to call themselves content providers.

I don't know if an artist can last by meeting the current public taste, the taste from the last quarterly report. I don't think you can last by following demographics and carefully meeting expectations. I don't know many lasting works of art that are condescending or deliberately stupid or were created as content.

Don't tell me I'm a brand. I'm famous and people recognize me, but I can't look in the mirror and see my brand identity.

Keep talking about brands and you know what you'll get? Bad clothes. Bad hair. Bad books. Bad movies. And bad records. And bankrupt businesses. Rides that were fun for a year with no employee loyalty but everyone got rich fucking you. Who wants that? The answer is purity. We can afford it. Let's go find it again while we can.

I also feel filthy trying to call my music a product. It's not a thing that I test market like toothpaste or a new car. Music is personal and mysterious.

Being a "content provider" is prostitution work that devalues our art and doesn't satisfy our spirits. Artistic expression has to be provocative. The problem with artists and the Internet: Once their art is reduced to content, they may never have the opportunity to retrieve their souls.

When you form your business for creative people, with creative people, come at us with some thought. Everybody's process is different. And remember that it's art. We're not crafts-people.

Sponsorships

I don't know what a good sponsorship would be for me or for other artists I respect. People bring up sponsorships a lot as a way for artists to get our music paid for upfront and for us to earn a fee. I've dealt with large corporations for long enough to know that any alliance where I'm an owned service is going to be doomed.

When I agreed to allow a large cola company to promote a live show, I couldn't have been more miserable. They screwed up every single thing imaginable. The venue was empty but sold out. There were thousands of people outside who wanted to be there, trying to get tickets. And there were the empty seats the company had purchased for a lump sum and failed to market because they were clueless about music.

It was really dumb. You had to buy the cola. You had to dial a number. You had to press a bunch of buttons. You had to do all this crap that nobody wanted to do. Why not just bring a can to the door?

On top of all this, I felt embarrassed to be an advertising agent for a product that I'd never let my daughter use. Plus they were a condescending bunch of little guys. They treated me like I was an ungrateful little bitch who should be groveling for the experience to play for their damn soda.

I ended up playing without my shirt on and ordering a six-pack of the rival cola onstage. Also lots of unwholesome cursing and nudity occurred. This way I knew that no matter how tempting the cash was, they'd never do business with me again.

If you want some little obedient slave content provider, then fine. But I think most musicians don't want to be responsible for your clean-cut, wholesome, all-American, sugar corrosive cancer-causing, all white people, no women allowed sodapop images.

Nor, on the converse, do we want to be responsible for your vice-inducing, liver-rotting, child-labor-law-violating, all white people, no-women-allowed booze images.

So as a defiant moody artist worth my salt, I've got to think of something else. Tampax, maybe.

Money

As a user, I love Napster. It carries some risk. I hear idealistic business people talk about how people that are musicians would be musicians no matter what and that we're already doing it for free, so what about copyright?

Please. It's incredibly easy not to be a musician. It's always a struggle and a dangerous career choice. We are motivated by passion and by money.

That's not a dirty little secret. It's a fact. Take away the incentive for major or minor financial reward and you dilute the pool of musicians. I am not saying that only pure artists will survive. Like a few of the more utopian people who discuss this, I don't want just pure artists to survive.

Where would we all be without the trash? We need the trash to cover up our national depression. The utopians also say that because in their minds "pure" artists are all Ani DiFranco and don't demand a lot of money. Why are the utopians all entertainment lawyers and major label workers anyway? I demand a lot of money if I do a big huge worthwhile job and millions of people like it, don't kid yourself. In economic terms, you've got an industry that's loathsome and outmoded, but when it works it creates some incentive and some efficiency even though absolutely no one gets paid.

We suffer as a society and a culture when we don't pay the true value of goods and services delivered. We create a lack of production. Less good music is recorded if we remove the incentive to create it.

Music is intellectual property with full cash and opportunity costs required to create, polish and record a finished product. If I invest money and time into my business, I should be reasonably protected from the theft of my goods and services. When the judgment came against

MP3.com, the RIAA sought damages of $150,000 for each major-label-"owned" musical track in MP3's database. Multiply by 80,000 CDs, and MP3.com could owe the gatekeepers $120 billion.

But what about the Plimsouls? Why can't MP3.com pay each artist a fixed amount based on the number of their downloads? Why on earth should MP3.com pay $120 billion to four distribution companies, who in most cases won't have to pay a nickel to the artists whose copyrights they've stolen through their system of organized theft?

It's a ridiculous judgment. I believe if evidence had been entered that ultimately it's just shuffling big cash around two or three corporations, I can only pray that the judge in the MP3.com case would have seen the RIAA's case for the joke that it was.

I'd rather work out a deal with MP3.com myself, and force them to be artist-friendly, instead of being laughed at and having my money hidden by a major label as they sell my records out the back door, behind everyone's back.

How dare they behave in such a horrified manner in regards to copyright law when their entire industry is based on piracy? When Mister Label Head Guy, whom my lawyer yelled at me not to name, got caught last year selling millions of "cleans" out the back door. "Cleans" being the records that aren't for marketing but are to be sold. Who the fuck is this guy? He wants to save a little cash so he fucks the artist and goes home? Do they fire him? Does Chuck Phillips of the LA Times say anything? No way! This guy's a source! He throws awesome dinner parties! Why fuck with the status quo? Let's pick on Lars Ulrich instead because he brought up an interesting point!

Conclusion

I'm looking for people to help connect me to more fans, because I believe fans will leave a tip based on the enjoyment and service I provide. I'm not scared of them getting a preview. It really is going to be a global village where a billion people have access to one artist and a billion people can leave a tip if they want to.

It's a radical democratization. Every artist has access to every fan and every fan has access to every artist, and the people who direct fans to those artists. People that give advice and technical value are the people we need. People crowding the distribution pipe and trying to ignore fans and artists have no value. This is a perfect system.

If you're going to start a company that deals with musicians, please do it because you like music. Offer some control and equity to the artists and try to give us some creative guidance. If music and art and passion are important to you, there are hundreds of artists who are ready to rewrite the rules.

In the last few years, business pulled our culture away from the idea that music is important and emotional and sacred. But new technology has brought a real opportunity for change; we can break down the old system and give musicians real freedom and choice.

A great writer named Neal Stephenson said that America does four things better than any other country in the world: rock music, movies, software and high-speed pizza delivery. All of these are sacred American art forms. Let's return to our purity and our idealism while we have this shot.

Warren Beatty once said: "The greatest gift God gives us is to enjoy the sound of our own voice. And the second greatest gift is to get somebody to listen to it."

And for that, I humbly thank you.

Article 7. Courtney Love

1. Why does Love call the way the major record companies do business "piracy"?

2. Why do artists need the major record companies? Put another way, why do artists sign such terrible deals with the record companies?

3. Does public taste account for what we get to hear, or do the record companies decide what we get to hear? If so, how?

4. According to Love, how will Napster or other file-sharing programs benefit artists?

5. According to you, how might Napster or other file-sharing programs benefit audiences?

6. To what in particular does Love attribute Napster's success?

7. Will less good music be created, as Love suggests, if you take away the incentive of money for the musicians themselves?

8. Why did RIAA take Napster to court?

9. According to Love's vision, how will the new global music market work?

10. What do you feel is the greatest potential for this new world of online music distribution?

11. WRITE a short essay discussing the competing visions of the music industry outlined by Frith (Article 6) and Love. Where, in your opinion, does the future lie?

Rock and the Facts of Life

■■■

Charles Hamm

When I arrived at Princeton University to begin work on a Ph.D. in musicology in 1957, with a life-long interest and involvement in various genres of American music, I discovered that:

> All books, monographs, editions, periodicals, and other materials considered necessary for successfully completing the degree had been collected in a large study-seminar room. . . . The word "canon" was never used then, but the ideology, though never articulated, could not have been clearer. The corpus of music and literature on music necessary for the pursuit of musicology was finite; it was all here in this room; and once our apprenticeship was completed and we moved out into the hard world of academia, our success would be measured by whether or not our own work would one day be brought into this room.
>
> The [general] stacks were situated just outside the door of our sanctuary, and occasionally, when none of my professors or fellow students was about, I would sneak a look at a score by John Cage or Charles Ives, or at a book about southern folk hymnody, or a bound collection of nineteenth-century sheet music. I felt like a teenager browsing through a collection of pornography.

What Wiley Hitchcock would later label "vernacular music" was no part of this canon, and my proposal to write a dissertation on nineteenth-century shape-note music was rejected out of hand. Dufay was acceptable, however, and my career as a scholar of Renaissance music was launched. But my interest in other types of music continued, and in 1970, as a member of a panel considering "Music and Higher Education in the 1970s" during a joint conference of the American Musicological Society and the College Music Society in Toronto, I suggested the following:

> The last five years have witnessed a period of intense and significant activity in American music almost without parallel in our history, a period of vitality and accomplishment in composition, performance, involvement of large and varied groups of people with this music, and above all of interaction

between music—and musicians—and the exciting and troubling events that have made this period such a critical one in American history. I am speaking not only of "art" music, of course, but the entire range of musical activity, from John Cage to Jimi Hendrix, Terry Riley to Simon and Garfunkel, Cecil Taylor to Roger Reynolds, Gordon Mumma to The Band to Merle Haggard to "Hair."

And I confess that I find it disturbing that none of this activity has been reflected in the publications and other official activities of the American Musicological Society, and very little of it in the teaching and other involvements of individual members of the Society.

[I] suggest that the most sensible and profitable course for musicology in the coming decade would seem to be one that would hold fast to the methods and accomplishments that have made our discipline one of the fastest-growing and most respected in recent decades, but at the same time to enrich and revitalize the field by constant broadening of the types of music, stylistic and chronological, that our scholars and teachers are concerned with, [and] to embrace whatever new methodology and aesthetic is necessary to deal sensibly with this larger and more varied body of material.

Reaction from certain musicological quarters was immediate and predictable. The then-director of graduate studies in musicology at Columbia University, a noted writer on Early Music, responded in the following issue of the same publication:

The gist of [Hamm's] argument is that one of the best musicological journals in the world, familiarly and affectionately known as JAMS, together with those who are sufficiently misguided to receive and read it regularly, should be censured for failing to give publicity to jazz, pop, rock, folk, tape, and trick music—if indeed the Muses have anything at all to do with these monosyllabic forms of activity. My reply is that neither the Journal nor its supporters deserve censure of any kind or degree; and it is no more incumbent upon them to feature the commercial

ephemerides that blight the artistic ecology of our sad planet than it is desirous that they should advertise cola drinks, greasy kid stuff, or the pill.

We are told that "many younger people of today . . . understand only too well the artistic, historical, and sociological value of this music." Younger than whom? Perhaps this sentence should read: "many immature quasi-illiterates understand perfectly the atavistic, hysterical, and social appeal of this noise." For noise most of it is, if you will consider the deafening volume at which most of it must be reproduced, and the incident of permanently damaged eardrums among its practitioners. As for hysteria, evidence is superabundant, ranging from a kind of mass hypnosis through drug-addiction to murder.

This same gentleman had written elsewhere, in response to a suggestion by Arthur Parris that Bach's cantatas were the "commercial" music of their day:

Bach wrote his cantatas as part of his duties as a director of music, and for the glory of Almighty God. Commercial music is written or improvised (the mode of transmission is of little importance) by decomposers as part of their duties as corrupters of public taste, and for the glory of the Almighty Dollar. . . . If Mr. Parris can honestly compare the finest of Binchois, or of any other great composer before or since, with the primitive vomiting noises wallowing in over-amplified imbecility that typifies most "commercial" non-music of today, he would be well advised to cure his addiction to value judgements.

It was in this climate that I made my first attempts to write about what I saw as America's "intense and significant" music of the 1960s and its interaction with "the exciting and troubling events" of the day. There was no literature in my own discipline to guide me. I knew some of the writing on "mass culture" by Adorno and other sociologists, but I couldn't imagine that this dour, elitist, negative approach, exhibiting an almost total lack of familiarity with the music in question, could be fruitful. Journalistic writing by David Ewen and his peers seemed equally unpromising, as did the growing body of sociological "youth and leisure" literature, since it seemed to me that popular music cut a much wider swathe in American culture. So I struck off essentially on my own, at first. My first attempts were shots in the dark, guided only by the germ of a conviction that popular music should be approached as a complex field encompassing composers, performers, audiences, the music industry, the media, and the state.

"Rock and the facts of life" was first delivered as a lecture during the winter of 1970–1, at Brown University and elsewhere. It seemed pointless to offer it to a musicological journal, so I turned to my friend and then-colleague Gilbert Chase, one of the great iconoclasts of the day, whose seminal book *America's Music: From the Pilgrims to the Present* had rekindled and broadened my interest in American music of all kinds. Characteristically, Gilbert not only accepted the article for his Yearbook but defiantly placed it as the first item in the next volume.

For those who don't remember, or weren't around, Hayakawa, a college professor in California, rose to political power as a proponent of "law and order" and received wide media coverage in the late 1960s as a forceful opponent of that state's rampant student activism. Though Hayakawa doesn't acknowledge it, the title of his article invokes Sigmund Spaeth's *The Facts of Life in Popular Song.*

S. I. Hayakawa, in an article called "Popular songs vs. the facts of life," explains that he is very fond of jazz and sometimes listens to popular music also, but he finds the latter disturbing. He recalls that Wendell Johnson, in *People in Quandaries*, isolated a disease infecting American society that he labelled IFD: Idealization (the making of impossible and ideal demands upon life), Frustration (as a result of these demands not being met), and finally Demoralization (or Disorganization, or Despair). The products of our popular culture are some of the chief carriers of this disease. Citing lyrics of songs by George and Ira Gershwin, Rodgers and Hart, Irving Berlin and the like, Hayakawa says that popular music is concerned

almost solely with idealized romantic love. He contrasts this with the lyrics of some of his favorite blues, particularly those of Bessie Smith, in which a much wider and more realistic range of what can happen between a man and a woman is portrayed—happiness, unhappiness, despair, loneliness, desertion, unfaithfulness, tenderness, and earthy passions. He concludes that blues show a willingness to acknowledge the "facts of life," suggesting, though he does not develop the point, that these "facts" include not only a wider spectrum of love but other matters as well. Citing Kenneth Burke's description of poetry as "equipment for living," he ends by saying:

> If our symbolic representations give a false or misleading impression of what life is likely to be, we are worse prepared for life than we would have been had we not been exposed to them at all. . . . Hence the question arises: do popular songs, listened to, often memorized and sung in the course of adolescent and youthful courtship, make the attainment of emotional maturity more difficult than it need be? . . . Cannot our poets and our songwriters try to do at least as much for our young people as Bessie Smith did for her audiences, namely provide them with symbolic experience which will help them understand, organize, and better cope with their problems?

Hayakawa, writing a decade after the end of World War II, cites songs from the 1920s and 30s, the period of his youth, when he himself was in a formative and impressionable period. One wonders if the songs popular some fifteen years later, when he wrote his article, were similar. To test this, I went to *Billboard* magazine's weekly listing of the most popular songs, based on record sales and other data. Assuming that it took perhaps a year for Hayakawa's article to be written, submitted, accepted, set, proofread, and published, I went back a year from the date of publication of the article, to the chart for the week of 8 May 1954 for a sample of what was in fact popular when he was writing. The ten most popular songs were:

1. Wanted   *Perry Como*
2. Make Love to Me   *Jo Stafford*

3. Cross Over the Bridge   *Patti Page*
4. Oh, Baby Mine   *Four Knights*
5. Young at Heart   *Frank Sinatra*
6. Secret Love   *Doris Day*
7. Answer Me, My Love   *Nat King Cole*
8. A Girl, A Girl   *Eddie Fisher*
9. Here   *Tony Martin*
10. Man with the Banjo   *Ames Brothers*

This list does indeed verify Hayakawa's thesis, and makes possible some amplification of it. With one exception, these songs deal with romantic love from the point of view of the mores of American white middle- to upper-class society: one man seeking one woman, going through difficulties and perhaps even heartbreaks in his search, but eventually attaining his goal, and with it lasting happiness. If there are other aspects of the man-woman relationship, they are scarcely hinted at here. If there are any other issues in life, this body of music is silent about them.

Hayakawa was concerned only with the lyrics of these songs, not with the music. If he had been, he could have pointed out that the homogeneous nature of this repertory extends to the music itself. The songs all sound alike. Each was sung by one singer, or occasionally a small vocal group, to the accompaniment of an orchestra dominated by strings but making some use of winds and brass. Each uses the same melodic style (diatonic, tonal, and heavily dependent on sequential writing) supported by a common harmonic style (thick, lush chords—tonal but liberally sprinkled with post-Debussyian seventh and ninth chords). Each is written in precisely the same form, in the same meter, moving at more or less the same tempo. A person whose knowledge of music was derived from this repertory would have a remarkably limited view of the potential of the art.

Hayakawa was correct. Whether or not he was listening to these or any other popular songs in 1954, his thesis that popular music gave a narrow and distorted view of reality, that it was not facing up to the facts of life, was a sound one.

At the time that Hayakawa was writing his article, ten years after the end of World War II, Eisenhower was president, America was engaged in the Cold War, politicians and would-be politicians were making capital of Communist-hunting in and out of government, and with a few exceptions Americans felt it in their best personal interests to go along with the internal and foreign policies of the government, to fit into the life style appropriate to their social and economic class, to conduct their lives so that they were moving towards maximum material gain, and to avoid any behavior or expression of beliefs that might impede their attainment of this goal. High school and college students seemed content to play the role of careless, uninvolved, transitory people, with responsibilities, decision making and involvement in the problems of the country off somewhere in the future. Deviation in belief and behavior among them was largely confined to a rather small group, mostly male, often on the fringe of criminal activity, almost all of them the children of families low in the economic scale of the country. The image of America as a benevolent, righteous nation dispensing impartial justice at home and abroad was rarely questioned or even examined, at least by those people in the groups and classes that listened to popular music.

One of the most convincing parts of Charles Reich's *The Greening of America* is his characterization of this period in American history, which he calls Consciousness II. He insists again and again that most decisions affecting the lives of Americans were made by the institutions of the country (political, religious, educational, economic, social), that people were under the impression that they were offered freedom of choice but this choice was from among options that were essentially the same. He illustrates this paradox of a choice that is no choice by his infamous peanut butter diatribe: American housewives going to a supermarket in search of peanut butter have a choice of different brands bearing different labels in differently shaped containers, but inside everything is essentially the same; and a person wanting something genuinely different, such as peanut butter that has not been homogenized, cannot find it, because a decision has been made that American peanut butter is homogenized.

A more telling example of this point is the situation with popular music of the time. Someone dependent on the large radio stations or certain types of record shops had a choice of what he listened to, a choice among Perry Como, Doris Day, Frank Sinatra, and Pat Boone, but in terms of musical style and content of lyrics this was a very narrow choice. Popular music was the music of middle- and upper-class white Americans, by and large, the people who held positions of power in financial, political, religious, and educational institutions; the people who listened to this music were the children of both groups, who would eventually succeed them. This music offered no view of life in America that questioned the way things were going. Of course there was jazz, blues, country music, and folk music of many sorts, and much of this music was bitterly critical of one aspect or another of American life—of the kind of life that many people were forced to live. But this was the music of minority groups, and the hard facts of life, of poverty, of repression, of apparently inescapable unhappiness, were unknown or ignored by the people who listened to Perry Como and Eddie Fisher, who heard in this music nothing that disturbed their limited and unrealistic view of what was and was not happening in the country. Bob Dylan said:

> Rudy Vallee. Now that was a lie, that was a downright lie, Rudy Vallee being popular. What kind of people could have dug him? . . . If you want to find out about those times and you listen to his music you're not going to find out anything about the times. His music was a pipedream. All escapes.

That's not completely true, though, because you *can* find out something important about those times from listening to such music. You can find out that the people who produced and consumed popular music were shielding and shielded from any contact with reality that might conflict with a certain narrow view of life in America. You can find out that the function of this music was clearly *not* to provoke or stimulate any thoughts or discussions of alternate ways of viewing American society.

Hayakawa's article was probably conceived in 1954; mine was first delivered as a lecture in May of 1970. Conditions in the United States were dramatically different then. The first gen-

eral student strike in the history of American education had closed or at least impeded operation of most American colleges and universities: the strike triggered by President Nixon's decision to send troops into Cambodia and the killings of students at Kent State and Jackson State. This strike was of course no isolated, impulsive happening. It came at the end of a decade of involvement by students and other young people in protests against the Vietnam War, attempts to focus attention on and seek solutions to racial discrimination, concern with the environment, and opposition to laws and practices that seemed discriminatory. The American student with his serious involvement in such matters and his insistence on being in the middle of—and if possible shaping—political and social matters, would have been almost unrecognizable to his counterpart in 1955.

And his music would have seemed equally curious. Here is the list of the top most popular songs for the week ending 9 May 1970, the week of the strike. The list is again taken from *Billboard*.

1. American Woman   *Guess Who*
2. ABC   *The Jackson Five*
3. Let It Be   *Beatles*
4. Vehicle   *Ides of March*
5. Spirit in the Sky   *Norman Greenbaum*
6. Love or Let Me Be Lonely   *Friends of Distinction*
7. Everything is Beautiful   *Ray Stevens*
8. Instant Karma   John Lennon
9. Turn Back the Hands of Time   *Tyrone Davis*
10. Reflections of My Life   *Marmalade*

Comparing this list with the one from 1954, two things stand out in shocking contrast. First, the subject matter of the lyrics: only one or two deal with romantic love. The most popular song, "American Woman" by the Canadian group Guess Who, is a naive but direct criticism of some aspects of American life: "American woman, stay away from me . . . I don't need your war machines, I don't need your ghetto scenes. . . ." "Spirit in the Sky" and "Let It Be" are religious songs, and "Instant Karma" reflects the curious, highly personal religious mysticism of John Lennon. "ABC," done by a black group, deals with love—sex, rather—in a teasingly erotic fashion not unlike some blues. "Vehicle" speaks of the risks of accepting rides with strange men in large new cars. "Everything Is Beautiful" praises tolerance by offering as its main theme the notion that anything can be beautiful "in its own way." "Reflections of My Life" is quite remote from blues, musically, but offers a view of life as a difficult and troubled journey that Hayakawa would have had no difficulty in relating to the "truths" of black music: "Oh my crying, feel I'm dying, Take me back to my own life. . . . The world is a bad place, a terrible place to live, Oh but I don't want to die. . . ." If anyone was listening to the radio this week, he would have been exposed to songs that gave a wide variety of views about life and love.

From a musical point of view, each one of these songs is different from any other one in sometimes small but often great matters of style. Four are done by solo artists, six by groups of differing sizes. The instrumental backing ranges from the percussion of "Instant Karma" through the standard rock ensembles of amplified guitars and percussion of "American Woman" to the studio orchestra, with strings, of "Reflections of My Life." Harmonic style is sometimes simple, diatonic, tonal, and triadic, with reference either to rock simplicity ("American Woman") or country-music simplicity ("Spirit in the Sky"); sometimes it derives more from gospel and rhythm-and-blues style ("Everything is Beautiful"); sometimes its reference is more to the popular music of Hayakawa's time, as in "Reflections of My Life." Melodic style is equally varied: in "American Woman" it is repetitious, fragmented, declamatory and almost non-melodic; "Everything Is Beautiful" has a simple, symmetrical, almost folk- or child-like tune; "Let It Be" has a flowing, balanced, diatonic, sequential melody; the long-spun, legato line of "Reflections of My Life" is almost operatic. There is an equally wide range of musical forms in this collection of pieces.

Thus listeners in 1970, even those who listened only to stations playing the most popular songs, were offered the sort of choice in musical style and content that had not been available in 1954. Millions of Americans, most of them young, were listening to songs concerned with a wide variety of subjects, many of them dealing with political and social issues of the day, many of them at variance with the view of American life offered by popular songs several decades earlier.

Just as the events of May 1970 were merely episodes in a chain of events stretching back at least a decade, so the songs popular that week represented no sudden new development but rather a continuation of currents that had been flowing for some time. It is not the intent of this article to discuss in any detail the history of popular music of the past decades. I will merely point out what is obvious to anyone who has been in any way involved with this music: since the mid-1950s, elements have been pouring into popular music that had not been found in it before. They have come from black music, country music, folk music of various types, art music, electronic music, and rock 'n' roll (itself indebted to black and country music). Some have come in directly, as songs in one or another of these styles that have become popular, other elements have been diluted or filtered or mixed with other styles. In sociological terms, popular music has been infiltrated by music from some of the minority cultures of our country, and this music has brought with it not just its sound, but in its lyrics the attitudes towards life prevalent in these subcultures. The main audience for popular music has been the young and the relatively affluent, the white middle- or upper-class youth. The infiltration into their popular music of music from various minority groups and subcultures, with the views of American society as seen through the eyes of these people, has exposed them to facts of life not habitually acknowledged in this layer of American society. What are these facts of life? Charles Reich says:

> The very first thing that began to happen when rock came in on a mass cultural level was it started to say "we feel lonely and alienated and frightened" and music had never said that before. Blues has always said it. . . . But white people were told how happy, how romantic, how nice, how smooth the world was. And that didn't reflect the truth.
> Then all of a sudden there was Elvis Presley singing about "Heartbreak Hotel"

full of lonely people, and he said no matter how full it is, when you get there you're lonely, because none of these people can communicate with you and you can't communicate with them. . . . So the first truth of rock, the first big communication, was to say things aren't that good.

This may not have been the first thing that rock said, but it did say, often, that the world is full of lonely, unhappy people, that lives can be or become tragic, that all people do not have an equal opportunity for happiness. Popular music of the past decade has seen a long parade of characters whose lives have gone in directions never hinted at in the songs done by Patti Page or Doris Day: the Beatles' "Eleanor Rigby," Simon and Garfunkel's "The Boxer," Bob Dylan's "Like a Rolling Stone," and the down-and-out aging hoofer in "Mr. Bojangles" by the Nitty Gritty Dirt Band.

Probably the first thing that rock said that "white music" had not said was that there is a physical side to love in addition to or in place of the sentimental, romanticized view of love portrayed in earlier popular music. The first wave of rock 'n' roll, in the mid-1950s, was certainly not characterized by lyrics of profound intellectual or sociological value. To the contrary, the words were unimportant. What mattered, what was different (and shocking to many people), was the feel, the beat, the excitement of the music itself, the unabashed movement and sensuality of the sound. As Dylan says:

> You gotta listen to the Staple Singers, Smokey and the Miracles, Martha and the Vandellas. That's scary to a lot of people. It's sex that's involved. It's not hidden. It's real. It's not only sex, it's a whole beautiful feeling.

Elvis Presley could be added to that list, and the Rolling Stones, Sly and the Family Stone, Jim Morrison and the Doors, Ike and Tina Turner, and scores of other individuals and groups. And hundreds of songs that have been played on the Top Forty stations and risen in the charts, dealing in open and vivid fashion with the physical side of love.

Another thing that rock has been saying for some time now is that war is unhealthy for children and other living things. Bob Dylan's "Blowin' in the Wind" was written long before there was any mass opposition to the war among the young people of America. It is difficult to say if the anti-war songs of the past decade had a direct influence on swinging the sentiment of a high percentage of young Americans against the war or if this sentiment was developing anyway, but certainly the songs and also the lives of such artists as Dylan and Joan Baez have played a role in solidifying—if nothing else—the beliefs of millions of people on this matter. The earliest anti-war songs were in the stream of folk-oriented music flowing into popular music in the early 1960s, but eventually music in other styles echoed this sentiment: basic rock, which initially and for many years was politically and ideologically neutral; black music (one of the most bitter outbursts against the war was Edwin Starr's "War," in what might be called a gospel-rock style, which rose to the top of the charts in late 1970); the music of such a popular solo artist as Donovan; and, finally, even white country music. The twentieth song on the *Billboard* chart for the week of 9 May 1970 was Johnny Cash's "What Is Truth?," in style exactly what would be expected of this long-popular country singer, in content a condemnation of the hypocrisy of Americans who hide tolerance of war and repression and intolerance of people whose views and appearance differ from their own behind their own notion of what is "American."

Still another fact of life dealt with again and again in music of the last decade is that drugs have become part of American life. There is no reason to belabor this point at this date. Recognition of the fact that lyrics of hundreds of songs of the past decade make reference to drugs, their use and effects has spread even to network television newscasts—and even to the office of the Vice President of the United States. Some of the songs are sympathetic to the use of drugs, some are not, most simply accept the fact that there is a drug culture in the country.

There are songs that deal with ecology, politics, old age, historical characters, humor, religion, patriotism, family relationships, the treatment of the American Indian—indeed, with an ever-expanding range of topics.

The matter is quite simple. Hayakawa complained that popular music offered a narrow, unreal view of life, that it did nothing to prepare its consumers for what life was like outside the fantasy world of this music. He called on "poets and songwriters" to create music that would provide "symbolic experiences" to help Americans "understand, organize, and better cope with" the world they face. But he could not have guessed how quickly and effectively his call would be answered. Beginning almost exactly in the year of his essay a succession of artists—most of them drawing on the music of one or another of the minority cultures of America—began producing songs suggesting that life was difficult, unpredictable, potentially tragic and lonely, sensual, humorous, exciting, and filled with experiences that families, churches, and schools had not prepared Americans for. This music often suggested that justice was not always administered in an impartial and humane way in America, that economic and military policies were sometimes determined by factors other than moral principles. Bob Dylan, Joan Baez, Bo Diddley, Elvis Presley, Peter, Paul and Mary, the Beachboys, Little Richard, Chubby Checker, the Beatles, Simon and Garfunkel, the Jefferson Airplane, the Grateful Dead, Frank Zappa and the Mothers of Invention, the Rolling Stones, Jimi Hendrix, Joni Mitchell, Phil Spector, Jim Morrison and the Doors, Janis Joplin, and dozens of other individuals and groups began offering "symbolic experiences" that gave young Americans a sort of preparation for life that their parents and grandparents had not had. Movies, some novels, and journalism have been saying some of the same things, but music has been the most popular and influential art in changing the consciousness of a generation of Americans.

Hayakawa went on to become a college administrator. A television newscast sequence of several years ago caught him perched atop a car, wearing a tam, facing a crowd of angry, hostile students intent on forcing changes in educational and governmental policies. These students were a new breed in America, with

attitudes and opinions quite different from those held by students in Hayakawa's day. They were aware of many facts of life not known to earlier generations of students. Much of this information had come from the music that had been popular during their formative years.

A Note on the Title of this Essay

Certainly not all the music mentioned above is rock. I have used it as a convenient term for a large, varied body of music. When popular music began to change dramatically, in the mid-1950s, the first group of songs to break in style and content with earlier popular music was rock 'n' roll, and a second major innovation came in the 1960s with West Coast and English rock, as opposed to rock 'n' roll. Other types of music also figured in the revolution of popular music. But they were all indebted to rock either stylistically or because it first opened the door for different kinds of music to enjoy the commercial popularity previously possible only for the sentimental ballads discussed at the beginning of this article. To put it another way, "rock" in my title should be understood as "rock 'n' roll, rock, and other kinds of music, mostly derived from the music of one of the minority cultures in America, that have become part of and revolutionized the popular music scene in America." But that would have been too long a title.

Epilogue

Changing attitudes of young Americans and the part that popular music has played in this have not gone unnoticed by the American government. Seventy-five radio executives were summoned to Washington in January of 1971 for an expression of concern from the Nixon administration about the airing of songs with lyrics making reference to drugs. On 5 March 1971 the Federal Communications Commission issued a "public notice" on the matter, reading in part: "Whether a particular record depicts the danger of drug abuse or, to the contrary, promotes such illegal drug usage is a question for the judgment of the licensee." It goes on to say that someone in a position of responsibility at each station should be expected to make such a judgement, and if this is not done, "it raises serious questions as to whether continued operation of the station is in the public interest. In short, we expect licensees to ascertain, before broadcast, the words of lyrics of recorded musical or spoken selections played on their stations."

Nicholas Johnson, an FCC commissioner who dissented from the notion of preparing and circulating such a notice, gave more information about its background in an interview over KSAN-FM in San Francisco:

> The thing I find most ominous is that the presentation we received was put together by the Pentagon for the President, and this Defense Department briefing on song lyrics in fact used a lot of lyrics that aren't talking about drugs at all—they're anti-war songs or songs attacking the commercial standards of society, the standards of conspicuous consumption.

Reaction to the notice was varied. Some stations, particularly the FM rock stations, seemed to ignore it and continued to play the same music as before. Some of the large commercial stations were more cautious though. WLS, the most powerful Top Forty station in Chicago, immediately began playing an unprecedented number of "souvenirs," or songs popular in other years, and those selected steered clear of controversial subject matter. A study of the weekly charts in the several months after publication of the notice shows a dramatic drop in songs dealing with drugs, and a similar drop in the number of songs dealing with war or the sensitive social issues of the day. It is not clear at this moment if the action by the government will have any long-range effects; there is sentiment that the notice could not withstand a court challenge. Whatever the outcome, the government of the United States has made it perfectly clear that it is not happy with a situation whereby popular music disseminates certain opinions and facts of life.

Article 8. Charles Hamm

1. What are the Top Ten singles for the week closest to the one during which you read this article? Do these reflect the "facts of life" today? Why, or why not?

2. How would you characterize the difference between the lyrics of most popular music of the first half of the century and the lyrics of the blues?

3. How would you characterize the difference between the lyrics and music of most popular music of the first half of the century and the lyrics and music of rock circa 1970?

4. How would you characterize the difference between the lyrics and music of rock circa 1970 and the lyrics and music of rock today?

5. What are some of the themes rock raised that had not been seriously raised in popular music before?

6. According to Hamm, consumers of popular music had very little range of choice in the 50s. Is there more choice today? Why, or why not?

7. Is innocence still possible in rock?

8. How did popular music shape America's conception of the world in the 50s? the 60s? How about today?

9. What effect do you think the anti-racism and anti-war songs of Dylan and others had on America?

10. Take two songs, one from the 60s and one from the last decade. Discuss how they reflect the political and social issues of their times.

11. Hamm's discussion of government efforts to influence radio and keep drug songs off the air has a peculiar resonance with more recent efforts by the White House under Bill Clinton to promote anti-drug messages via television by paying the producers of shows that promote such messages (in an apparently equally devious manner: see the *Washington Post*, 14 January 2000, p. A1). Is this Big Brother? But if education is the only way to beat drugs, should we blame the government for trying to do *something*? Take one side of the issue and argue for it.

Part

III

Technology

19 January 1967:
'Well I just had to laugh . . .'

George Martin

Very few Beatles tracks are more original, or more gripping when you first hear them, than the next track we recorded for the new album, 'A Day In The Life'.

John brought his initial ideas to Paul and they sat down in the music room upstairs at Cavendish Avenue to work together on the song. I must confess that I had always thought, like most people, that the lyric *'he blew his mind out in a car'* referred to the death of Tara Browne, who was a close friend of John and Paul. Not so. Some Beatle analyst somewhere had put two and two together to make five. In fact the marvellous lyrics that the composers concocted had nothing to do with a car crash. But it was a drug reference, as was *'I'd love to turn you on'.* They had been imagining a stoned politician who had stopped at some traffic lights.

John's inspiration for lyrics often came from things he had observed or read.

> I was writing the song with the *Daily Mail* propped up in front of me on the piano. I had it open at their News in Brief, or Far and Near, whatever they call it. There was a paragraph about 4000 holes in Blackburn, Lancashire, being discovered and there was still one word missing in that verse when we came to record. I knew the line had to go, 'Now they know how many holes it takes to . . . the Albert Hall.' It was a nonsense verse really, but for some reason I couldn't think of the verb. What did the holes do to the Albert Hall? It was Terry Doran, a friend, who said, 'Fill the Albert Hall.'
>
> —Hunter Davies, *The Beatles* (Heinemann)

Bob Dylan was a strong influence on John. He showed that you could write lyrics that had punch, pith, and bite; that reflected, say, intimate personal experience—or political anger.

Other influences on John, sworn to by those who were closest to him, are harder to detect. John's guardian Aunt Mimi, for instance, once said she 'saw a lot of Balzac in John's songs . . .' Whatever can she have meant by that? She tells us, in Ray Coleman's biography of him, *John Winston Lennon*, that her ward had a voracious appetite for Honoré de Balzac's short stories, a large collection of which could be found on her bookshelves.

Well, Balzac's use of realism—historical, economic, social—is all-pervasive. Realism is a way of making his stories seem true-to-life, among the other things he uses it for. Here is John on the same subject:

> Rock 'n' roll was real, everything else was unreal. And the thing about rock 'n' roll, good rock 'n' roll, whatever 'good' means, is that it's real, and realism gets through to you despite yourself. You recognise something in it which is true, like all true art.
>
> —*John Lennon Remembers*

He certainly wrote about the thing that was most real to him, which was his own everyday life. And 'A Day In The Life' is a pretty good example of that.

In the early days John wrote some very effective, very simple songs based on the guitar, but his love of word-play, his sheer sense of fun with words, was always right to the fore when he was composing. From the very start of his musical career he was writing down the verbal fireworks displays that would later become his funny, witty books—and his songs.

I remember a trip to the seaside at Margate, where the Beatles were appearing in some variety theatre or other—it might even have been an appearance on the end of the pier—these were very early days! Judy and I had gone along to keep them company. John was scribbling down the beginnings of *In His Own Write* into a little notebook; silly words, nonsense words like Edward Lear's *Jabberwocky*, warm and readable and entertaining. Judy looked over at what he had written, liked it, and started reading it out loud. Judy Lockhart Smith's upper-crust accent, reading John Lennon's words, made everybody fall around with laughter:

> It were a small village, Squirmly on the Slug, and vile ruperts spread fat and thick amongst the inhabidads what libed there.
>
> One victor of these gossipity tongues had oft been Victor Hardly, a harmless boot, whom never halmed nobody. A typical quimmty old hag who spread these

vile ruperts was Mrs Weatherby—a widow by her first husbands.

> 'They're holding a Black Matt down at Victor's pad,' was oft heard about the village—but I never heard it. Things like this were getting Victor down, if not lower . . .

The Beatles were beside themselves, rolling about as these strange half-nonsensical words came tripping off Judy's silken tongue. It was then that we all realized how kooky, how entirely off-the-wall some of John's thoughts and lyrics really were; and that Jabberwockyness developed enormously as time went on. The lyrics were a more important part of John's songs than they were in some of Paul's. It would be silly to say that John ignored the music, but the lyrics generally drove the composition of his songs.

We did a first run-through of 'A Day In The Life' on 19 January, with Paul on piano, John singing and playing acoustic guitar, Ringo on bongo drums, and George on maracas. On that first take, John counts in on the tape by saying, 'Sugar plum fairy, sugar plum fairy . . . ' which does nothing to diminish the belief that he was taking drugs on *Pepper*! (A 'sugar plum fairy', in drugs parlance, is the person who brings you your dope, or whatever.) This first stab at recording 'A Day In The Life' concentrated on the bare bones of the song, which so far had no middle section.

Track 1: basic backing of the entire record: piano, guitar, maracas and bongo.

Track 4: John's vocal, already with heavy tape echo on it. John always hated his voice, always wanted something done to it. In this case he said he wanted to 'sound like Elvis Presley on "Heartbreak Hotel"'. So we put the image of the voice about 90 milliseconds behind the actual voice itself. As the voice goes past the record head it obviously records. The playback head is situated after the record head, so you hear the voice later. In the old days, we used to do tape echo that way: take the voice off the playback head and feed as much as you wanted of it back into the record head. (Nowadays you do it by means of digital delay.) Geoff Emerick says that to get that echo, he fed John's vocal on to a mono tape machine, then took the output of that, because the record/replay heads on a mono machine were separate, then fed it back on itself over and over again until he got a twittery kind of vocal sound.

John was listening to this in his cans, and hearing so much distortion on his voice made him feel really happy. John's liking for stupendous amounts of echo stemmed from his early teens. When he was very young and learning to play the guitar, a maddened Aunt Mimi would frequently banish him to the porch of their Menlove Avenue semi. The porch's acoustics gave his voice a natural echo, and he grew up used to it sounding like that. It seemed normal to him. John also discovered early on in his career that tape echo came in handy for his sense of rhythm: when the delay on the tape was right it helped him to keep time.

In fact, John's voice on this first run-through was marvellous, as usual.

We still had to include a middle eight on the song, so we recorded our roadie Mal Evans on this track, Track 4, as well. His job was to count down the twenty-four bars in the middle of 'A Day In The Life' that were still blank. Why twenty-four bars? Why not?

John asked Paul if he could think of anything for this yawning space. Paul had written a scrap of song, which John liked: 'Woke up, fell out of bed, Dragged a comb across my head . . . ' So they agreed to put that in. But it was Paul's idea to have something really tumultuous on the song, something that would whack the person listening right between the ears and leave them gasping with shock. He didn't know quite what it was he wanted, but he did want to try for something extremely startling.

Paul was carrying the backing to the song on the piano. During that twenty-four-bar gap, all you could hear was his piano banging away, with a lot of wrong notes, some of them deliberate, the dissonance increasing as his playing got more frenzied towards the end. To keep everyone together, and so that we would know when we were due back into the song proper again, Mal Evans counted the bars out loud. This sounded very dull—'one, two, three . . . '—so we put an increasing amount of tape echo on his voice, too: at the end there was a tremendous amount of reverb on it.

Just to make sure that everyone knew when to restart, we added an alarm clock at the end of the final bar. This was really not trying to be clever, not at this stage, anyway. We were a bit bored and the clock was just a little joke. As it happened, the alarm going off fitted perfectly with the lyrics that started Paul's middle section to the song, 'Woke up, got out of bed . . .' so the bell stayed in.

Before we went home, John overdubbed a couple of extra vocal takes, on Tracks 2 and 3 (we had his original vocals on Track 4). In the end, I selected Track 2 as the best, but while John was recording on Track 3, Paul added some heavy piano chords at the beginning of the song, a few bars in, at the end of the instrumental introduction.

We came back to the song the following day, a Friday. I mixed everything down on to two new tracks of a second tape: all the piano, guitar, maracas, bongo drums on Track 1, and a mix of John's various vocals, complete with echo, on Track 2. In some cases we double-tracked John's voice, overlaying what we'd recorded the previous day. Next, Paul overdubbed his bit, laying down his vocal for the new middle section of the song, the 'Woke up, got out of bed . . . ' segment. Rather than use up any further tracks on this new, mixed-down tape, I dropped Paul's vocals on to it, in between John's own. All the vocals were now on one track.

Once he had listened to them, Paul thought he could make a better job of his vocals, and he had another stab at them on 3 February. Track 3 we used up recording Ringo's wonderful drum-track combination of bass drum, cymbals and famous tom-tom sound, which he re-recorded that evening, and Paul laid down his bass guitar track at the same time. Ringo and Paul recorded simultaneously, because I didn't want to waste any more precious tracks.

We had been keeping Track 4 of this second tape free for orchestral work, but Paul used it to lay down still more piano.

On analogue tape, every time you transfer one track to another, you multiply the signal-to-noise ratio. Dirt comes up, all the background hiss and audio clutter, and this noise multiplies by the square of each tape-to-tape transfer. Two copies create four times the amount of noise; a third generation increases the noise by nine times! So I had to be very disciplined in keeping the track usage together.

Producers today would be horrified at such restrictions—they are used to recording every sound on its own track. Because of this good-housekeeping requirement, Paul would be aware that if he made a mistake with his bass playing, he might be ruining a great take from Ringo; and Ringo would be thinking the same thing about his own performance. It was an added spur for them to play well. . .

> I joined the band because they were the
> best musicians around in Liverpool, and
> I wanted to be with that . . .
> —Ringo, *South Bank Show*

By the time we finished the session on 20 January (in fact it was about 1 a.m. on the 21st), I loved the song: John's dry, deadpan voice, Paul's bouncy middle segment acting as a foil to that, and I really liked the chords that got us back to John's section, which was in a different key. We were not sure then what else we wanted to do to it, so we left it for a bit, to think. We often worked in this way, starting something new to give us more time on another song in progress. It was the painter laying aside the canvas, starting a new work, then coming back to the first work afresh, able to see at once what was good or bad about it, and what needed to be done by way of improvement.

In the meantime, Paul came up with the idea of the *Sgt. Pepper* title song, which we began recording.

I needed a break from recording 'A Day In The Life', in any case, because I had to do some scoring for orchestra. The Beatles had come to me and said they wanted a symphony orchestra. Paul fancied the idea more than the others. 'Nonsense,' I replied. 'You cannot, cannot have a symphony orchestra just for a few chords, Paul. Waste of money. I mean you're talking about ninety musicians! This is EMI, not Rockefeller!' Thus spake the well-trained corporate lackey still lurking somewhere inside me. Yet my imagination was fired: a symphony orchestra! I could see at once that we could make a lovely sound.

I thought very hard. The song did need a grand flourish of some sort. This crazy idea might just work. We had never used a sym-phony orchestra before; we'd used a string quartet, an octet, the odd trumpet or a sax section, so the notion of a great leap forward into a full-sized orchestra was very appealing—and kind of logical. It is one of the biggest toys you can play with. But ninety musicians would be expensive; too expensive.

'What do you want this symphony orchestra to do, exactly?' I asked, stalling for time. I really was not sure that it had been properly thought out. But Paul had been listening to lot of avant-garde music by the likes of John Cage, Stockhausen, and Luciano Berio. He had told John he would like to include an instrumental passage with this avant-garde feel. He had the idea to create a spiralling ascent of sound, suggesting we start the passage with all instruments on their lowest note and climbing to the highest in their own time.

I decided half a symphony orchestra would do—smaller string section, single woodwind and brass—and settled on forty one musicians. Cheeseparer! Honour was satisfied, but I knew it was of little use telling them to improvise. They were used to working from written parts, no matter how strange. I suppose it was difficult for the Beatles to fully understand that. They had never needed a note of written music in their lives. Why should anyone else? Of course, if we had approached the symphony musicians in those days without a prepared score they would have laughed us out of court.

When I sat down to write the score, I realized that John had not come up with anything for the first few notes the orchestra would have to play, after he stops singing, 'I'd love to turn you on . . .' He sings this line in a very characteristic manner, the tune wavering between semitones. This, I thought, would be a great phrase to echo, so I wrote a very slow semitone trill for the strings, bowing with a gentle *portamento* and increasing gradually in frequency and intensity. This gives a suitably mysterious effect, making a good introduction or bridge to the now famous dissonant orchestral climb that is unique to this song.

The twenty-four-bar gap we were now going to fill needed notes, even though the 'slope up'—the climb—did not. What we did over those twenty-four bars was to instruct each musician to begin by playing the lowest note on their instrument (as quietly as they could!), and to finish at the end of the final bar by playing their loudest and highest note. The main thing I had to accomplish with this score was to give the orchestra signposts: the twenty-four vacant bars took quite a long time to get through—about forty seconds—and the musicians were supposed to be gradually sliding up, very, very slowly, and as smoothly as possible. The strings weren't playing notes, just slithering away.

The woodwind and some of the brass instruments had to play distinct notes, although some players could lip, rather than tongue, their notes to make a smoother transition from one note to the next. At each bar line I marked in an approximation of where each musician should be, like so many way points along a musical route.

When it came to the recording, I was counting out the bars as they went through them, so they knew that when they got to bar six, for example, they should be at A flat, or whatever. Having given them the score, I had to tell them how to play it. The instructions given, though, shook them rigid. Here was a top flight orchestra, who had been taught all their lives by maestros that they must play as one coherent unit. I told them that the essential thing in this case was *not* to play like the fellow next to them! 'If you do listen to the guy next to you,' I told them, 'and you find you're playing the same note, you're playing the wrong note. I want you to go your own way, and just ignore everything else; just make your own sound.' They laughed; half of them thought we were completely insane, and the others thought this was a great hoot.

As the Beatles had never had a symphony orchestra before, they wanted to make the recording a special occasion. 'Will you wear evening dress,' they asked me, 'and will you get the orchestra to wear evening dress?'

'Are *you* going to?' I asked.

'Yeah,' they came back. 'We'll do it!'

'All right,' I said. 'If you wear evening dress, I'll wear evening dress.' They didn't, of course, but they wore their version of it: outrageously flamboyant floral costumes. Not quite *Sgt. Pepper* costumes, but very flower power. For some reason known only to himself, Paul, for example, arrived wearing a full-length red cook's

apron, which clashed horribly with his purple-and-black sub-Paisley pattern shirt!

They were determined to have a party, so they invited along a few of their mates—only about forty or so, including Mick Jagger, Marianne Faithfull, Pattie Harrison, Brian Jones, Simon Posthuma and Marijke Koger of the design team the Fool, Graham Nash, all of them wearing long, multicoloured flowing robes, stripy 'loon' flared pants, brilliant waistcoats, gaudy silk neckerchiefs, love-beads, bangles, baubles, badges and bells. Mingling discreetly in amongst all this unisex hippy flamboyance was Judy, wearing, of all things, a tweed suit—very fashionable!

People were running around with sparklers and blowing bubbles through little clay pipes. There was a funny rich smell in the air, which may of course just have been the joss-sticks that were burning all over the place . . .

It was a happening. As soon as the recording got under way, I told the flower-children to sit around the walls and behave themselves; and, just like good children, they did!

After I'd run the orchestra through to make sure they had got their notes right (or should that be wrong?), I went back to Geoff in the control room to make sure he was getting it all down on tape. Also, I had a technical worry: I'd already filled up my tracks and wanted to be sure that the rough synchronization Ken Townsend had been fixing up for us was ready.

I was in the control-room with Ken and Geoff for about ten minutes. When I came back into the studio the party was in full swing. The Beatles had been among the evening-dressed orchestra handing out carnival novelties. Erich Gruenberg, leader of the second violins, was playing with a monkey's paw on his bowing hand and wearing coloured paper spectacles. David McCallum, the leader of the London Philharmonic (and father of *The Man From U.N.C.L.E.* actor), was wearing a very large red nose. There was a balloon on the end of the bassoon, which went up and down as the bassoonist played. I stared at it all and started laughing. It was a riot. 'Come on,' said Paul, 'join in, George. Let's have some fun.' 'But Paul,' I replied. 'You said fun is the one thing that money can't buy!'

Of course, in its way it was fun. But at the back of my mind—all the time—was the thought that this was a very expensive way of letting our hair down. I had an urge to get this thing structured, a fear that it might break down into complete chaos and the whole effort go to waste. I was pretty nervous, in short.

During the course of my career I had either worked with the forty-one musicians we used that evening, (they were all men—women had not then been liberated in the world of British classical music), or I had met them some other way. Erich Gruenberg, for example, had won the Max Rostal prize when we were both at the Guildhall School of Music. Knowing them all so well definitely helped calm my nerves on this particular occasion!

All the time, Geoff was tweaking away at the studio's in-built 'ambiophony' system, which instantly fed the music back through the hundred speakers spaced around the studio walls to create a customized—and highly amplified—sound.

We recorded 'A Day In The Life' on three different tapes; very unusual for the Beatles. Tape 1 had the rhythm backing and John's voice. We dubbed those down on the second day, adding extra vocals, together with the first track of the orchestral recording. Then we added four more tracks of the orchestral recording, making five in all. The orchestra actually performed five separate times, and each time they were distinctly different. On the last take of all, for example, there is lots more timpani—drums—than on the previous attempts.

When we were satisfied with the orchestral material, we had to synchronize it with our original four-track master. This was difficult, to say the least. Nowadays it is dead easy to lock tapes together in perfect synchronicity: an electronic code called SMPTE, currently indispensable in recording studios, does the job. In 1967, though, nothing like that existed. There was the hit-or-miss method of jump-starting the tape machines together by hand. But this was extremely difficult to pull off, and usually meant the speeds of the two machines would differ by a tiny but noticeable amount. And sooner or later they would drift out of time. This was where Ken Townsend and his ingenuity came in. Realizing I would be in trouble, he had been cooking up a scheme to run the machines in synch. And it almost worked!

Ken's idea was to run an identical 50-hertz pulse to the capstans of each tape machine so that one would kick-start the other, in exactly the same way, every time, on time. Even with that achieved, the process of hitting the same exact musical start-point on two separate machines was still a matter of trial and error. It required a great deal of patience and understanding. I kept the Beatles well away from the scene of the action while all this was going on!

Looking back on those ancient times, I still wonder at the primitive state of our art. If I were to do it again, I would have no qualms about booking the entire London Symphony Orchestra several times over. But I am not convinced it would be any more effective: our string and sealing-wax methods did the job all right. If you listen closely to the original recording, though, you can hear the orchestra going in and out of time. It's not their bad playing—just our crude synchronization system falling down on the job.

'A Day In The Life' was something special, even before it had the orchestral orgasm grafted on to it. It was and is a great song. John's vocal on it really did something for me. I was always enormously captivated by his voice, and on this track it is at its best. I miss hearing that voice terribly.

Having done all the orchestral bit, we wanted something to finish off the song. When you reached that high note at the close of the orchestral sequence you were left hanging there; the song needed bringing sharply back down to earth. What we required, I thought, was a simple yet stunning chord. Something very, very loud, very resonant. But what would give us that resonance? I decided to try out a notion which went back to the recording of 'Tomorrow Never Knows'; the '4000 monks' ploy. I had always thought that the sound of a lot of people chanting a mantra was impelling and hypnotic. 'Why don't we make a chord of people singing, to make a noise like a gigantic tamboura?' I suggested. 'Get them to sing all the basic notes, with maybe a few fifths in between, and track them, over and over and over again, to give it depth?'

So we did that, and there is a tape of it at Abbey Road in the vaults. If I had had 4000 people available to sing, it might have worked. As it is, the noise that came out the other end is absolutely pathetic! I had eight or nine people, multiplied four or five times. Nobody had enough breath to hold the chord beyond about fifteen or twenty seconds, so it petered out, anyway, long before it should have done.

So we moved smartly on to a second idea: a gigantic piano chord. You get a wonderful sound from a piano if you let the overtones work. Try it for yourself: if you have a piano in your house, open the lid wide, press down the sustain pedal (the right one), lean over, and shout. You will hear the piano singing back to you all the little notes that are in your voice. When there are many of those overtones working against each other, they generate extra frequencies, so-called 'beat' frequencies, which give a wonderful kind of rolling effect. Now multiply that a thousand times . . .

We managed to scrape together three pianos. After a few hilarious practice shots, Paul, John, Ringo, Mal Evans and I crunched down on the same chord as hard as we could. You can hear my voice on the master tape counting in to the chord, so that everyone hits it at exactly the same time.

If you recorded a heavy chord strike like that on a piano without any compression, you would hear a very, very loud note to begin with, but the die-away would be very quiet. We wanted the first impact of the chord to be there (although not overbearing), but the decay to be very loud. (Compression takes the impact of the note, absorbs it like a shock absorber, then brings the volume back up quickly to compensate.) As the chord started to fade, Geoff Emerick raised the gain gradually, to keep it singing on. At the end of the note, forty-five seconds into it, the volume level on the studio amplifiers was enormous.

Everybody had to be terribly quiet. If anybody were to have coughed, it would have sounded like an explosion. As it is, on the special Ultra High Quality Recording edition of *Sgt. Pepper*, you can hear the Abbey Road air-conditioning system purring away in the background as Geoff opens the volume faders to the stops at the very end of the die-away. That's how we got the famous piano chord.

Article 9. George Martin

1. What influence did technology have on the making of "A Day in the Life"?

    - orchestra
    - echo effects
    - alarm clock

2. Does the energy of rock suffer in *Sgt. Pepper's* as a result of the Beatles' immersion in the studio. That is, are the studio tricks "music"?

3. Describe the difference between the Beatles' approach to music making and that of the classically trained musicians used on *Sgt. Pepper's*.

    - jamming out v. sheet of music

4. What is indeterminacy?

5. What did you find surprising about the techniques used to create "A Day in the Life"?

6. What can you infer about the personalities and musical interests of the Beatles?

7. Why is *Sgt. Pepper's* considered a work of genius?

8. Choose one genre or style and discuss the impact of technology upon that style.

The Fuzz

■ ■

Michael Hicks

Just as rock singers refracted their voices into multiple personalities, rock guitarists transformed their instruments into surrogate singers. Aided by new technologies, rock guitarists exchanged the instrument's historically slight musical presence (with delicate timbres, low dynamics, and rapid decay) for a new, overwhelming presence (with rough timbres, loud dynamics, and the ability to sustain—or, as Paul McCartney puts it, to "flow"). At the center of the exchange was a warm, powerful, sonorous sizzle known as "fuzz."

Fuzz grew inevitably from the peculiar sonic world of mid-twentieth century popular music. In the 1920s and 1930s brass players in Duke Ellington's band popularized the "growl and plunger" style of playing, a raucous mimicking of the vocal roar. By humming, flutter-tonguing, or literally growling while playing, players like Bubber Miley and Cootie Williams got tones that sounded like a controlled, distorted scream. In rhythm and blues music of the 1940s and 1950s (and Motown and Memphis soul recordings of the 1960s) saxophone players routinely emulated the trumpet growls of those earlier players; by combining various hard mouthpieces and stiff reeds, by blowing with extra force, and using the techniques of Miley, Williams et al., tenor and baritone saxophone players could make the already noisy timbre of their instruments sound even more ragged. Such effects allowed a player to transcend conventional virtuosity—as measured in notes per measure—in favor of a more primal, direct expression. This so-called "boot" style of tenor saxophone playing offended many purists. One complained that through it "a player of very little improvisational talent can achieve instant success with the mob by playing three or four successive choruses on one note. Provided, of course, that he heightens the impression of inspirational fervour by blowing himself blue in the face and marking time like an epileptic sergeant major." Despite such cynicism, the boot style prevailed.

Although boot style began by imitating the roar and buzz of rhythm and blues singers, saxes and voices gradually achieved a symbiosis. The techniques of each reinforced the other—as Screamin' Jay Hawkins explained, his ambition was to make his voice "duplicate the sounds I got off a tenor sax." But sax playing required immense physical effort, as did the roar and buzz of the singers. In all cases the sound was terse and forced, as though great strength and resistance were required to give them utterance—and they were. During the early years of rock 'n' roll, vocal and saxophonal distortion complicated the sonorous edge of the music—an edge reinforced by the sizzle of ride cymbals, snare drums, and, occasionally, maracas.

That complex of distorted sound complemented the technological basis of the rock 'n' roll industry. Most people learned rock 'n' roll through the radio, where signals competed with one another for dominance of a particular wave band. The music often came through a sieve of white noise and electrical hum that made almost any instrument or voice seem to buzz. (This was especially true of the earliest rock 'n' roll, which first appeared on some of the weakest, most remote stations.) And the records that were broadcast had their own distortion. Not only was the music typically recorded at high levels on hissing tapes, but repeated playings wore out the vinyl and made the music even fuzzier. As the predominant media of rock 'n' roll, broadcasting and recordings turned what was once an undesirable flaw into the essence of the sound. That essence signified raw power, survivability in the face of interference.

In the early twentieth century dance bands began to include guitars with brass and saxophones, a situation that created a serious imbalance of sonority: the guitar was essentially a quiet instrument, the saxophone a loud one. So in the 1920s manufacturers experimented with guitar "pick-ups," magnetic coils that could vibrate sympathetically with the instrument's strings. In 1931 Rickenbacker issued the first commercial electric guitar, a lap-held Hawaiian model resembling a long-handled frying pan. Later in the decade, the National and Gibson companies devised more conventionally shaped electric guitars. Meanwhile, some players began to make their own electrics by installing pickups in their acoustic (i.e., non-electric) guitars. Finally, Les Paul and Leo Fender dispensed with the guitar's resonating cavity entirely, building the first solid-body electric guitars in the late 1940s and early 1950s. With their new designs (and more refined pick-ups) both makers hoped to increase the instrument's tonal "purity," reducing the hum and buzz of older electrics. In the process, they redefined the electric guitar by demonstrating to the public what electrical engineers had long known: the strings of an electric guitar provoked electrical impulses directly.

Trying to keep their prices competitive, makers of electric guitar amplifiers used low-cost "P. A. grade" transformers in their equipment. At normal volume levels these transformers distorted the signal about 5 percent. But when pushed beyond their capacity—"overdriven"—the distortion levels rose to around 50 percent. Black rhythm and blues guitarists usually could afford only the smallest, least powerful amps. At the same time they had to play in some of the noisiest venues. Although evidence is scarce, Robert Palmer quite plausibly suggests that bluesmen such as Muddy Waters were forced to overdrive their weak amplifiers "just to cut through the din." But at some point, probably in the late 1940s, the bluesmen discovered that, by turning their amplifiers up louder than they were designed to be, they could make the guitar's timbre resemble the raunchy, distorted timbre of boot saxophone playing.

Many of the records made at Chess Studios in Chicago in the late 1940s and early 1950s captured the sound. In Howlin' Wolf's "All Night Boogie" (1953), for example, Willie Johnson's overdriven electric guitar dovetails with a similarly overdriven miked harmonica and Wolf's own "overdriven" voice to paint a perfectly consistent timbral painting. (Sun Studios in Memphis harnessed a similar sound, particularly in the guitar playing of Pat Hare.) In such cases the capturing of live distortion on records required careful engineering, since the studios wanted to faithfully document the distorted sound of the *guitars*, rather than distort the *recording* by overdriving the microphones. Whether the listener would have discerned the difference is hard to say.

Writers generally point to Guitar Slim as the electric guitarist who played the loudest, most distorted blues of the early 1950s. Playing through the P.A. system (rather than through a separate guitar amplifier), Slim always kept his guitar at maximum volume—with the club doors open to attract customers. His maniacally distorted sound became legendary, not only through his performances but also through recordings like his hit "The Story of My Life" (1954), in which the guitar solo, rather than the vocal—perhaps for the first time on a rhythm and blues record—seemed the real point of the song.

Like electric blues players, rock 'n' roll guitarists almost inevitably overdrove their amplifiers, trying to project their music above the sound of drums and talkative audiences. Chris Dreja of the Yardbirds assessed the situation of many groups and their early stage equipment: "God, it was basic. Between the five of us we must have had all of twenty watts. It was so quiet I could hear myself hitting the strings of my electric guitar." Nevertheless, upon hearing such groups in England in 1962, Muddy Waters remarked, "Those boys were playing louder than we ever played."

If overdrive was almost inevitable, some kinds of distortion were not. In many cases, accidental (and later, deliberate) damage to amplifiers enhanced the fuzzy sound. As early rock 'n' roll groups toured from club to club, the frequent moving made it likely that the cardboard cones of the speakers might be torn, or tubes damaged. In most such cases a band would simply replace the damaged part or, if times were good, buy a new amplifier. In March 1951, however, Willie Kizart tore the woofer cone of his amplifier while driving to a Jackie Brenston recording session at Sun Records in Memphis. There was neither time nor money to repair it. When the group arrived at the session with the broken speaker, producer Sam Phillips stuffed a newspaper and a sack into the hole and decided to record with the speaker as it was. Tellingly, Phillips remarked, "It sounded good. It sounded like a saxophone." Phillips added that he wanted the "authentic" sound that the broken equipment gave the recording: "If they had broken-down equipment or their instruments were ragged. . . . I wanted them to go ahead and play the way they were used to playing. Because the *expression* was the thing."

The result was a simple boogie record noteworthy only for the strange fuzzy sound of the guitar, which (like the saxophones in many New Orleans recordings) merely doubled the walking bass line, outlining the triads of the chord progression. Brenston and Phillips entitled it "Rocket 88," a tribute to the 1950 V-8 Oldsmobile 88, which was advertised as "the lowest priced car with 'rocket' engine." While the tune was unimaginative, the novel guitar sound attracted many listeners.

Five years later, another amplifier accident reshaped the sound of Johnny Burnette's Rock 'n' Roll Trio. Guitarist Paul Burlison recalls that the strap of his Fender Deluxe amplifier broke before a show in Philadelphia, dropping the amp on the floor. "When we started playing, it sounded fuzzy, but it wasn't enough to stop the show. So Johnny looked around and grinned and we just kept on playing. When I got back to the dressing room I took the back off the amp and looked at it, and what had happened was one tube had slipped about halfway out. So I pushed the tube back up and it worked fine; pushed it back down and it'd get fuzzy." Burlison's accident had not produced permanent damage, as Willie Kizart's had. Instead, the loose tube had shown him a method of tone production that was controllable (i.e., it functioned as a rheostat). It was an effect that could be switched on and off, irrespective of volume or speaker quality. In that regard, it directly foreshadowed the fuzz "controls" of the early 1960s, by which players could turn the distortion on and off with a switch.

Burlison decided to use the fuzzy guitar sound on the group's 2 July 1956 recording session for two songs, "Blues Stay Away from Me" and "Train Kept A-Rollin'." The distortion was barely noticeable in the former song, but in the latter it was prominent. As with "Rocket 88," the distorted guitar was the record's principal novelty. As "Train Kept A-Rollin" became widely known, according to Burlison, "I had engineers calling me from all over the country asking how I got that sound." Despite the interest, Burlison exploited the sound in only one subsequent recording—the calypso-based "Touch Me" (recorded March 1957).

The role of the distorted guitar in "Blues Stay Away from Me" and "Touch Me" resembled its role in "Rocket 88": it was an interesting coloration of standard guitar ostinati. It outlined the chord, provided some contrapuntal interest, and articulated the beat. But in "Train Kept A-Roll-in'" Burlison uses the guitar primarily to make loud low-register plunking sounds, effectively turning it into a powerful percussion instrument. The rapid reiterations create texture and sonority for their own sake, without a conventionally functional harmonic, melodic, or bass-foundational role. Dominating the other elements of the recording, the fuzz guitar seems to emulate the chugging of a train at full speed.

Still one more accident produced another legendary distorted guitar solo. In Bobb B. Soxx and the Blue Jeans' "Zip A Dee Doo Dah" (1962), Billy Strange's electric guitar part leaked into some of the live mikes around the studio, creating a strange, growling sound. Producer Phil Spector thought it a flaw, but left it in. As engineer Larry Levine explained, Spector "didn't care what the break was gonna sound like. We played a full chorus before we got to the break, and you don't sell a song with a solo on a break." But he did not envision how important a voice the lead guitar was coming to be. Described by one writer as a "tinny coil of disembodied noise," Strange's guitar break became the record's most important contribution to rock—the first Top 10 fuzz guitar solo.

In the late 1950s some electric guitarists began to damage their equipment deliberately in order to create fuzz. This happened mainly among *instrumental* rock 'n' roll bands, who continued the tradition of the rhythm and blues dance bands of the 1950s. Early rock 'n' roll instrumental bands featured saxophone, but in the late 1950s guitars took over. Without words or a lead vocalist, instrumental hits often used gimmicks and sound effects to make them memorable.

In 1958 guitarist Link Wray drove a pencil through the speaker of his amplifier before recording a new instrumental record. According to rock lore, he damaged the speaker specifically so that the guitar sound would better represent the aggressive sound of a gang brawl—a "rumble." (The truth, however, is probably that the damage came first and the record's title, "Rumble," came later. The daughter of the owner of Wray's record label said that the untitled recording reminded her of the rumble scenes in *West Side Story*, then a Broadway play. Hence the title.) "Rumble" is a slow, twelve-bar

(sometimes eleven-bar) blues, in which the guitar primarily plays slow, clanging chords. Given its relatively innocuous harmonic and rhythmic content, "Rumble" clearly demonstrates how one could produce a Top-20 hit with little else but the sheer sonority of fuzz. Wray tried (unsuccessfully) to duplicate the success of his first fuzz record in recordings that include "Raw-Hide" (1959), "Big City after Dark" (1962), "Black Widow" (1963), and "Deuces Wild" (1964).

But Wray did inspire many guitarists of the early 1960s to follow his example. Larry Parypa of the Sonics, for instance, "was always fooling around with the amps. . . . disconnecting the speakers and poking a hole in them with an icepick." Deep Purple's Ritchie Blackmore claims to have kicked in a speaker (ca.1960) in order to create a fuzz effect. Around 1963 Dave Davies of the Kinks took the 8-inch speaker of a 4-watt amplifier and "proceeded to cut [it] into ribbons with a razor blade. Then I patched it up with Sellotape and stuck a few drawing pins into it." He set this on top of his 30-watt amp, keeping the smaller one at full volume and the bigger one as low as possible.

With this arrangement the Kinks produced their initial hits "You Really Got Me" and "All Day and All of the Night" (1964), which together codified the technique of "power chords"—overdriven barre chords that were given a terse, grunting quality by relaxing the left hand just enough after each strum of the right so that the ringing of the strings would be stopped. This was the guitar equivalent of the stopped articulation of raucous soul saxophone players, except that it now applied to whole harmonies.

While many guitarists wanted at least an occasional fuzz effect, few could afford to wreck their amplifiers to get it. One alternative was the recording studio: guitarists could distort their sound by recording with the input levels in the red—even if their own amplifiers sounded clean. But this still left the problem of playing fuzz in concert. The solution came from the so-called "fuzz box," a small accessory to a guitar amplifier that severely "clipped" the peaks of the instrument's natural wave form.

While most of the documentation on early fuzz boxes has been discarded or lost, the earliest such devices appear to have been introduced in 1962. The best known from that year was the Maestro Fuzztone FZ-1, a triangular brown footswitch that resembled a door stop. It allowed guitarists to control not only the tone of the instrument (i.e., treble and bass), but also the amount of distortion. Unsure of how to market such a device, the Gibson company (a distributor for Maestro) told prospective buyers that the Fuzztone would make a guitar sound like a cello!

The Ventures—the most popular rock 'n' roll instrumental band—probably used the Maestro device in "The 2,000 Pound Bee," parts 1 and 2, recorded in October 1962. In part 1 of this track the group plays a modified twelve-bar blues, with a single riff transposed to the level of each of the harmonies; part 2 differs only slightly. Nothing distinguishes this novelty record except for the fuzzy guitar that plays the melody. Although "2,000 Pound Bee" sold relatively poorly (only the B-side made the charts—Number 91), the Ventures continued using the fuzz box on other records. In their *Surfing with the Ventures* album (1963) they use some degree of overt distortion on nine of the twelve tracks—sometimes in accompanimental patterns, but usually in the lead melody (most prominently in the track "Barefoot Ventures"). Two subsequent singles—"Journey to the Stars" (1964) and "Pedal Pusher" (1965)—use heavy fuzz. But both failed to chart.

The "2,000 Pound Bee," however, had caught the attention of three British guitarists and a young technician who lived near them. In 1963 seventeen-year-old Roger Mayer began working for the British Admiralty as an assistant experimental officer in sound and vibration analysis. While evaluating types of distortion for his job, Mayer tried to emulate and improve upon the Ventures' fuzz guitar sounds. Making fuzz boxes soon became his hobby. He gave some of them to his friends Eric Clapton and Jimmy Page, the latter of whom passed along a fuzz box to Jeff Beck. Other guitarists also took interest in the boxes. One, Jim Sullivan, became the first to use a Mayer fuzz box on a record—P.J. Proby's minor hit "Hold Me" (1964).

Jeff Beck joined the Yardbirds and used a Mayer fuzz box on one of his first recordings with the group. The three-pitch lead guitar riff of "Heart Full of Soul" (recorded February 1965) had originally been conceived for a sitar, and producer Giorgio Gomelsky hired two sitarists to play the riff at the recording session. But despite the exotic timbre, the delicacy of their sound and their rapid decay prevented the sitars from carrying the idea effectively. Beck suggested that with his fuzz box he could get an overtone-rich sound similar to that of the sitars, but with more volume and less decay. His version prevailed.

The Rolling Stones forcefully brought the fuzz box to public attention in their hit "(I Can't Get No) Satisfaction." Keith Richards recalls that his own three-pitch guitar riff for the song was "actually a horn [i.e., saxophone] riff," one that was "in essence not meant for the guitar." Richards used no fuzz for the riff in the first several takes of the song (made in spring 1965). But, as he explained, "that riff needed to sustain itself." A fuzz box provided the solution. Although Richards always considered the fuzz sound on "Satisfaction" a "bit of a gimmick," it generates much of the song's expressive power. As David Dalton put it, the distorted riff "balances neatly on the borderline of menace, arrogance and incitement"—traits that entwine with the lyrics and Jagger's delivery.

The music of "Satisfaction" oscillates between the two basic sonorities introduced in its opening. One is the grainy, medium-pitched buzzing and jangling blend of tambourine, snare drum, and fuzztone. The other is the smoother, darker sound of the bass. At the beginning of each verse, Richards switches off the fuzztone, and Jagger baby talks the line "I can't get no satisfaction," matching his vocal timbre to the bass and (now fuzzless) guitar. Then he and Richards sing the words "'Cause I try and I try and I try and I try," singing higher and louder until their voices recede into the recorded mix of instrumental timbres. At the highest sung pitch the voices closely resemble the fuzztone, which Richards then switches back on. Jagger sings solo for the duration of the verse, matching his voice to the fuzztone timbre. He begins the next verse in baby talk and the entire process begins again. The polar sonorities of the rhythm section remain constant, with the melodic bass distinctly separated from the mechanistic snare drum and tambourine. But electric guitar and voice modulate from darker, throatier sonorities to brighter, raspier sonorities, then back again.

In the wake of "Satisfaction," fuzz became a standard color in the palette of electric guitar sounds by late 1965. "Distortion" controls and switches appeared on amplifiers, "fuzz" knobs on guitars. Several electronics companies began to issue their own versions of the fuzz effects pedals—with names ranging from the "Distortion Booster" and the "Tone Bender" to more metaphorical titles, such as the "Astrotone" and the "Pep Box." One could hear fuzz guitar in everything from cheaply made garage band records to slick pop and even prime-time television themes.

By the end of 1966 the "distorted" sound of fuzz became a standard of stylistic purity—as suggested in the magazine *Popular Electronics*. For years the magazine showed amateurs how to build sound equipment that minimized distortion. Now an article suggested that fuzz was no longer a sign of damage but a hallmark of musical achievement: "As you listen to rock-'n'-roll by the big time performers, do you often wonder how they can get that fuzzy, raspy, piercing sound from an electric guitar while nonprofessional groups sound distinctively small-time?" The article went on to instruct amateurs how to build a device that would "sound as if [it] were tearing your speaker to shreds"—for less than three dollars.

The Seattle-born guitarist Jimi Hendrix turned fuzz from a mannerism into an art. In late 1966 he moved to London, partly because he wanted to learn how to make his guitar sound like Beck's in "Heart Full of Soul." Fortuitously, Hendrix met Roger Mayer after a January 1967 performance and experimented with some of Mayer's guitar effects-boxes in the dressing room. Thereafter, the two collaborated on fuzz and other effects until Hendrix's death in 1970. Mayer made over a dozen fuzz boxes for Hendrix, using several different designs customized to the sound Hendrix wanted. Hendrix became increasingly fastidious about fuzz; one of his road managers recalls him occasionally "screaming" that "this fuzz box isn't right" and trying several before he found the one with the right distortions. As the flamboyant and virtuosic Hendrix became the most influential rock guitarist of the late 1960s, he alerted listeners to a widening palette of fuzz guitar subtleties.

Through fuzz the guitar assumed a new identity in rock music. What was the model for that identity? Robert Palmer suggests that amplified guitar sonorities such as fuzz turned the guitar into a huge bell—a resonant, overtone-laden chiming sound, full of a "clanging" that "ritually invoke[s] sonic space." And this is precisely what Link Wray had created in "Rumble"—a massive, carillon-like instrument that made the guitar sound both majestic and ominous. By simply defacing his amplifier speaker, Wray seemed to intensify the natural overtones of metal strings, creating what Carlos Santana called distortion's "rainbow effect."

But there is ample historical evidence to suggest that distortion was designed to change the guitar into a saxophone—not just a sustaining instrument that can "solo" (a point that Palmer readily concedes), but a wordless variant of the buzzing, roaring voice that exemplified African-American ideals of singing as dramatic expression. While the saxophone required a huge amount of physical exertion and dexterity to produce its effects, the overdriven guitar made a similar sound with ease, as electrical energy supplanted bodily force. Players no longer had to coordinate throat, tongue, and lungs. Instead they could turn on a switch and pick the strings. One could play with the buzzing instrumental sound almost endlessly (the only limitation being the durability of one's fingers).

This transformation assured rock's connection to what in the early twentieth century was known as futurism—an aesthetic that glorifies the sounds of technology. In the early twentieth century it was the technology of machinery; in the late, the technology of electronics. Thus, Johnny Ramone explains that he "always wanted to get a sound like electricity" on his guitar; that fairly well sums up the futurist aesthetic. Moreover, futurism seeks to incorporate some of the inadvertencies of technology into its aesthetic—accidents, wear, breakage, ruin. Thus Andy Parypa proudly notes that his distorted playing made his group the Sonics sound "like a trainwreck"—a standard futurist image.

Nevertheless, fuzz imbued the electric guitar with a soul it had not had. As many guitarists have observed, distortion gave the guitar a sense of personality—it "enlivened" the sound, gave it "character," to the point where, as Eddie Kramer remarked, the particular distortion a player used became "synonymous" with his or her "individuality." In this way fuzz arose from both the western tradition of developing a "singing" tone on one's instruments and the African tradition of developing a distinctive "personal" sound on one's instrument. From the mid-1960s on, electric guitar players used countless variations on the fuzz idea to give themselves unique, inimitable basic sonorities.

Through fuzz, a guitarist could give his or her instrument a voice. It might be the transcendent, Middle-Eastern voice of "Heart Full of Soul," the brassy, urban voice of "Satisfaction," or anything in between. It might even be the voice of another species—the barking of "Train Kept A-Rollin'," the snarling of "Zip A Dee Doo Dah," or the buzzing of "2,000 Pound Bee." In every case, whatever the means of distortion, fuzz gave a guitar its own peculiar vocal "grain."

In the process, the guitar—once known as the "queen of instruments"—became an intensely masculine expressive tool. Through distortion its tone became, as one guitarist put it, "testosterone-laden." That pretense of virility in the sound of the guitar corresponded to the aggressive images in the titles of guitar instrumentals—gangfights, rockets, trains, buzzsaws, and 2,000-pound bees. The primary emotion was anger, a point observed even in Guitar Slim's overdriven playing, of which one observer commented "it really sounds like he's mad at somebody." The next generation found in fuzz the "overdriven-ness" of youth, the explosive hormonal diffusion in creatures whose social status was rigorously contained by their elders.

Through its aggressive, futuristic sound, fuzz was at the core of the machismo aesthetic of a new rock avant-garde—garage rock. Moreover, in psychedelic rock, the guitar would effectively exchange places with the voice, gaining its own multiple personalities through electronic special effects of which the fuzz box was only the beginning.

Article 10. Michael Hicks

1. Why was fuzz a characteristic element in all early rock?

2. Trace the development of the electric guitar to the early 1950s.

3. In their sound, what instrument did early rhythm-and-blues and rock-and-roll guitarists imitate?

4. Why did rock guitarists need to overdrive their amplifiers? When they did so, what did they discover?

5. How did accidental and deliberate damage to amplifiers contribute to the sound of early rock? Name an influential example of this distortion.

6. When and why was the fuzz box invented?

7. What song brought the fuzz-box sound to wide attention?

8. What was Jimi Hendrix's contribution to the sound of rock?

9. Write a short essay discussing what you feel are the two most significant technological developments to influence rock/pop music.

Part

IV

Drugs and Rock

Eight Miles High

Robert Palmer

"It was incredible because of the formlessness, because of the thing of people wandering around wondering what was going on . . . and stuff happening spontaneously and people being prepared to accept any kind of thing that was happening and add to it. Everybody was creating."
    Jerry Garcia, the Grateful Dead, on the first Acid Test, 1965

"Recently, it has become possible for man to chemically alter his mental state and thus alter his point of view. . . . He then can restructure his thinking and change his language so that his thoughts bear more relation to his life and his problems, therefore approaching them more sanely. It is this quest for pure sanity that forms the basis of the songs on this album."
    13th Floor Elevators, from the liner notes for their first album,
        The Psychedelic Sounds of the 13th Floor Elevators, 1966

"Psychedelic music is music that expands your awareness, your consciousness. It's that simple."

Phil Lesh, the Grateful Dead

"Nobody can define psychedelic music. Psychedelic is when the person that is listening to it is on acid."

Paul Kantner, the Jefferson Airplane

"Americans invented the blues: This is what we have got to be proud of. It ain't the nuclear stuff, it's not putting the man on the moon, it's the blues. And when the blues ran up against psychedelics, rock and roll really took off."

Ken Kesey, author and Merry Prankster

LSD-25 was a gift to the burgeoning youth culture of the sixties from a most unlikely Santa, the CIA. Originally synthesized in 1938, lysergic acid diethylamide, "acid" for short, was classified as a "psychedelic" or "mind-manifesting" substance after clinical tests discredited an earlier theory that it mimicked so-called psychotic states. Caught up in these clinical tests were several bright young men who later became "counterculture gurus," among them poet Allen Ginsberg and novelist Ken Kesey. If the CIA was disappointed that LSD proved ineffective as an agent of covert or psychological warfare—the effects were simply too unpredictable—the "guinea pigs" recruited for testing found other uses for it.

"I went to the Stanford Research Institute every Tuesday for many weeks," says Kesey. "They would give me one thing or another, which could be LSD-25, or LSD-6 or mescaline, or it might be a placebo; and they would pay me twenty bucks. There were about a hundred of us that went through the program. Not long after that, Ginsberg said this was all coming from the CIA, but nobody believed that, like nobody believed a lot of other conspiracy stuff."

When the experiments were called off, the guinea pigs revolted. "There is something very American about this," argues Kesey, who was a college athlete and wrestler. "When they said, 'Hey, we've got a new territory over there, and we'd like to have some explorers to go over and check it out,' it seemed like the most American thing to do—like crossing the continent in covered wagons, or going to the moon. Then after we'd come back and given our report to King George, the king said, 'Don't let anybody else go up there; I don't like the way these people look.' But the experiment was already in progress, and us guinea pigs decided, 'Well, if you guys don't have the balls to carry on with this, we'll do it on our own.' And it's still going on."

Kesey and various friends began throwing LSD "parties" in San Francisco's bohemian North Beach. Before long, the parties had become "happenings," the Kesey crew (which included fifties beat-movement avatar Neal Cassady, immortalized as Dean Moriarty in Jack Kerouac's *On the Road*) had dubbed themselves the Merry Pranksters, and a scruffy electric band had become an integral part of the proceedings. This was the Grateful Dead, one of those mixtures of schooled and self-taught musicians that often seems to make for a favorable group chemistry (no pun intended) in rock and roll. Like many of San Francisco's sixties rockers, Dead guitarists Jerry Garcia and Bob Weir had played folk music and bluegrass. (Their earliest musical involvement had been with fifties rock and roll.) Organist Ron "Pigpen" McKernan and drummer Bill Kreutzmann preferred hard-edged r&b. When Phil Lesh was

drafted by Garcia to replace an earlier bassist, he had never played the instrument before; *his* background was largely in classical and electronic music—and, according to Garcia, in big-band jazz.

Rock and roll has always thrived on a certain amount of musical diversity, most notably in the interaction of self-taught blues or country musicians with jazz-trained session players so characteristic of the fifties. But rarely had a rock or r&b band included musicians from so many different backgrounds, with such heterogeneous areas of expertise. In the sixties, such bands became the rule rather than the exception. In the case of the Dead, the diversity helped prepare them for a different kind of playing and a different kind of audience, beginning with the first of the "Trips Festivals" presented by Kesey and friends, which took place December 4, 1965, at a private house in San Jose. The LSD came free with the one-dollar admission; at the time, the substance was not illegal.

"Before, when we were playing the bars, what we did was basically r&b with a large amount of weirdness inserted into it," says Garcia. "We started as a dance band; when we took off from an r&b song on a twenty-minute improvisation, the bartenders loved us because the audiences would dance themselves silly and afterward they would be dying for a drink. But then we burnt out on the club scene and got involved in the Acid Tests. Since everybody paid their dollar to get in, including the performers, and nobody was coming to see *us*, we had maximum freedom; we could play absolutely anything, or nothing at all. Of course, we were experimenting with LSD ourselves. I don't think playing high ever yielded much of musical value, but it did instill in us a love for the completely unexpected. So right around then, the idea of having a set list, even having fixed arrangements, went completely out the window. We were playing to people who were taking LSD and dancing their hearts out, and it was easy, because we were playing from that flow."

Drugs and music making have interacted in a variety of ways throughout human history, but specific musical developments have rarely been attributed to the effects of drugs. Louis Armstrong's lifelong fondness for marijuana may have had something to do with his extraordinary sensitivity to tonal richness and detail, but nobody characterizes Armstrong's brilliant improvisations as "psychedelic" or "pothead" music. Heroin may have had something to do with the ability of modern jazzmen like Charlie Parker to reel off the most complex and rococo flurries of notes while maintaining an air of slightly bemused or disengaged "cool," but we don't call bebop "junkie jazz." Nevertheless, LSD is a special case, and not just because it is so much "stronger" in its effects than, say, THC, the psychoactive component in marijuana. From a pharmacological or medical point of view, the difference between the effects of smoking marijuana and taking a hit of LSD may be one of degree rather than kind. But an LSD trip, given a sufficient dosage and a lack of inhibiting factors (such as a chemical antago-nist), is quite capable of "shaking" an individual to the core of his or her being. It can be a life-changing experience, revealing (not merely "suggesting") that environmental and psycho-logical (external and internal) realities are not at all as they had seemed. The results can be personally empowering, or highly destabilizing, depending at least in part on the degree of un-derstanding and preparedness one brings to the experience.

"For some people, taking LSD and going to a Dead show functions like a rite of passage," says Jerry Garcia. "Each person deals with the experience individually; it's an adventure that you can have that is personalized. But when people come together, this singular experience is ritualized. I think the Grateful Dead serves a desire for meaningful ritual, but it's *ritual with-out dogma*. You know, we don't have a product to sell; but we do have a mechanism that works." Beginning around 1965, rock musicians made use of this working mechanism to explore their own relationship to music making, and the re-lationship of music to pure sound. LSD can pro-vide alternative modes of processing sensory input; "Feel purple! Taste green!" blared ads for *The Trip*, one of the first acid-exploitation B movies, written by a young Jack Nicholson. More to the point, one could "explore" appar-ently simple sounds, "get inside" them. "When you're high, you like to blow flutes and knock rocks together," says Kesey. "You like to listen to the purity of a sound."

LSD also seems to slow down the passage of time, or render it plastic. There is a tendency to perceive music more as a flow than as a lin-ear succession of discrete events or moments. The tripster/listener now "has the time" to ap-preciate sonic detail, the specific, sensuous tex-ture of each sound. A sound that is particularly rich in harmonic overtones, such as the buzz and shimmer of drone strings on an Indian si-tar or tamboura, may be especially appealing. But almost any sound can be interesting once one "takes the time" to examine it carefully. There is a sense of playfulness about all this; the musician and listener cooperate in the creation of a kind of virtual reality, a sonic play-pen in which sounds can be investigated and toyed with in a spirit of childlike delight and wonder.

This playful, plastic, participatory immer-sion in what we might call the sonic bath strongly suggests that a redefinition of music is in order: Music is simply organized sound, or more specifically, *sound organized by conscious-ness*. It follows that any sound can be musical as long as it is contextualized as such. This defi-nition may seem radical from a pop-music point of view, but it has been accepted in modern classical and avant-garde circles for years. "Noise music" was part of the anti-art program of Dada and the Futurists during the first two decades of the twentieth century. In the thir-ties and forties, Edgard Varèse, John Cage, and Harry Partch were composing with "noises" derived from specially constructed instruments or sound machines; "found" and electronically generated sounds on tape; and, in Cage's "Imagi-nary Landscapes," from radios tuned to differ-ent stations. In the late fifties and early sixties, composers such as Karlheinz Stockhausen re-fined the art of tape-collage while John Coltrane and La Monte Young, each in his own way, adapted the sonic drone and repeating melodic cycles of Indian and Arab music as a fresh for-mat for improvisation.

The spread of LSD from the CIA's "con-trolled experiments" into the culture at large undoubtedly accelerated the penetration of these and other rarefied influences in rock and roll. Bob Dylan led the way on the lyric-writing front, transforming what had largely been teen-oriented dance music with social and psychological resonances into a forum for "investigations into the nature of consciousness." But Dylan showed little interest in effecting a similarly radical transformation of the music itself, once his exploded song-forms gave him sufficient room in which to work. That task he left for others, and by 1965 there was no shortage of volunteers. Emboldened by the experience of LSD, encouraged by an audience that actually seemed to *crave* experimentation, a generation of rock and roll musicians embarked on a journey to the music's outer limits, and beyond.

From the very beginning, psychedelia was a cultural moment—in plain English, a fad—as well as a process of genuine musical innovation. The first rock and roll band to espouse the psychedelic cause openly was almost certainly Austin, Texas's 13th Floor Elevators, who were presenting their reverb-drenched r&b as a "quest for pure sanity" in 1965 and early 1966, before Kesey's Acid Tests, before "Eight Miles High" and *Revolver* and more than two years before the Grateful Dead's tentative first album. And already, in the band-written liner notes to *The Psychedelic Sounds of the 13th Floor Elevators*, their first album (released by International Artist [sic] of Houston in 1966), we find warnings about "those people who for the sake of appearances take on the superficial aspects of the quest." Various songs on the album are said to illustrate "the difference between persons using the old and the new reasoning. The old reasoning, which involves a preoccupation with objects, appears to someone using the new reasoning as childishly unsane. The old system keeps man blind to his animal-like emotional reactions. . . . The new system involves a major evolutionary step for man." This is Dylan's "Ballad of a Thin Man" ("Something is happening, and you don't know what it is/Do you, Mr. Jones?") writ large indeed, us versus them inflated into a gnostic cosmology in which the material world and its institutions incarnate darkness and death and only the Knowers are cognizant of the divine spark within.

This response to the psychedelic experience is interesting for several reasons. It is a direct response, as yet unmediated by the marketing efforts of Dr. Timothy Leary and other self-appointed tripster gurus. In contrast to

Leary's adumbration of Eastern reality maps such as the *Tibetan Book of the Dead*, it is a *Western* response, representing an insurgent strain of do-it-yourself spirituality and individual contact with the ineffable at least as old as Christianity itself. Finally, it is a response that needs to be factored into any genuine understanding of what went on in the sixties. For behind the media-friendly facade of peace, love, and flowers, the sixties were a period of violence, conflict, and paranoia, with battle lines being drawn in the streets. For every Woodstock, there was an Altamont, for every "All You Need Is Love" and "Sunshine Superman" there was an "Ohio" (on the shooting of demonstrating Kent State students by the National Guard) and a "Born under a Bad Sign." Given a choice between meditative quietism and rocking the foundations of consensus reality, rock and roll would almost have to choose the latter in order to remain true to itself.

If any single artist epitomized both the spirituality and the insurgency of the times, that artist was saxophonist John Coltrane. Though he entered the decade with impeccable jazz credentials and the blessings of his former employers Miles Davis and Thelonious Monk, Coltrane had experienced a spiritual awakening and began to view his music more as a "quest for pure sanity," a development that alienated the jazz traditionalists. A composer of gorgeously lyrical melodies, Coltrane increasingly used his precomposed themes as launching pads for no-holds-barred group improvisations, headlong leaps into the sonic bath. His example encouraged rockers in "the quest," inspiring ferocious outpourings of freely improvised "energy music." (Coltrane had investigated LSD himself and was responsible for turning other jazzmen on, most notably Ornette Coleman, who says Coltrane gave him his first "hit.") But Coltrane's most important contribution to the new rock was on a how-to, nuts-and-bolts level: He showed musicians how to improvise practically endless melodic variations by superimposing a variety of scales, modes, and textural variations onto a single root-chord or drone. This was an ingenious Western adaptation of the *principles*, as opposed to the merely exotic colorations, of Indian and Arabic music, which were the source for many of the scales or modes Coltrane employed. Rock musicians have rarely been comfortable with the complex, rapidly changing harmonies or chord sequences of conventional jazz and the Tin Pan Alley songwriting tradition; Coltrane opened up a world of possibilities beyond the major, minor, and blues scales that had long been the rockers' stock-in-trade, bringing extended improvisation within their grasp for the first time. Among the beneficiaries were guitarists such as Eric Clapton, Roger McGuinn, Jimi Hendrix, and Duane Allman—Coltrane freaks all.

The first "psychedelic" rock hit was the Byrds' "Eight Miles High," written in 1965 and released as a single in April 1966—the same month the Beatles recorded their first overtly psychedelic track, John Lennon's "Tomorrow Never Knows," later included on the *Revolver* album. At a press conference celebrating the release of "Eight Miles High," Byrds guitarist Roger McGuinn spoke at some length about the record's Coltrane influence. He was trying to emulate Coltrane's soprano saxophone style on his electric twelve-string guitar, he announced, right down to "the sound of valves [on the saxophone] opening and closing." What McGuinn apparently did not mention at the time was the source of the four-note melodic motif that leads from the opening vamp into the song proper and later recurs at appropriate intervals, lending this carefully thought-out composition an exceptional thematic coherence. The four-note figure was originally the opening phrase of Coltrane's composition "India."

Lyrically, "Eight Miles High" was a deliberately cryptic account of the Byrds' first visit to England. You had to be "in the know" to understand that, for example, the "small faces" referred to were actually an up-and-coming British band, or that the title was a reference to the cruising altitude of transatlantic flights. (The actual figure would be closer to "Six Miles High," but the Beatles had recorded "Eight Days a Week" and somehow "Eight" sounded more poetic. . . .) Unfortunately for the Byrds, the record ran afoul of one of those tiresome, periodic efforts to "cleanse" the airwaves, the target this time being overt references to drugs. A leading record-industry tip sheet identified "Eight Miles High" as a drug song and recommended that it be dropped from playlists; ra-

dio stations were happy to comply, and the de facto censorship undoubtedly prevented the record from becoming the hit it should have been (though it did climb to number fourteen on the *Billboard* charts). "If we'd wanted to write a drug song, we'd have written a drug song," McGuinn protested. More recently, David Crosby, one of the architects of the Byrds' forays into Indian music and Coltrane, asked rhetorically, "Did I think 'Eight Miles High' was a drug song? No, I *knew* it was. We denied it, of course. But we had a strong feeling about drugs, or rather, psychedelics and marijuana. We thought they would help us blast our generation loose from the fifties. Personally, I don't regret my psychedelic experiences. I took psychedelics as a sort of sacrament."

The Beatles' "Tomorrow Never Knows" also treated the psychedelic experiment as a kind of sacrament. But rather than construct his own scaffolding of metaphor and explication, Lennon in effect gave his endorsement to Timothy Leary's manual for tripping, based on the *Tibetan Book of the Dead*. A Tibetan Buddhist conception of the afterlife may or may not be an appropriate metaphor for what Westerners could have expected to encounter on LSD if left to their own devices. But this much is clear: The dialogue on psychedelics was now a media dialogue, one in which rock music would play a central role.

Musically, "Tomorrow Never Knows" was a truly revolutionary piece of work, the result of unprecedented studio experimentation. Tape loops were overlaid, piled one upon the other until the master tape was almost saturated. Guitars were distorted, fed back, speeded up, mixed with sounds made by wineglasses and other everyday objects. There was more Stockhausen than Coltrane in this "quest for pure sanity," but in another, more fundamental sense, "Tomorrow Never Knows" and "Eight Miles High" are very much alike. They exemplify the musical impact of the psychedelic experience on rock and roll before media stereotypes began to dictate what the with-it acidhead should see, feel, listen to, and wear. And, like most of the enduring rock and roll to have emerged from this particular moment in time, both records are built on inspired songwriting and craftsmanship. Even when the songs diverged radically from traditional song forms, the very conciseness of the pop singles format kept the sonic experimentation from degenerating into mere self-indulgence.

Many bands soon abandoned the singles format in favor of more open-ended explorations, resulting in "profound" album-length noodling to no particular purpose. Today, these records are little more than quaint period pieces—a criticism that can arguably be leveled at that sacred cow of psychedelia, *Sgt. Pepper's Lonely Hearts Club Band*. Although the album remains a marvel of the record-making process, achieving unheard-of effects without recourse to today's computer-assisted multitracking technology, the effects are not always organic. One often has the impression that these effects are cosmeticizing or disguising the songs' superficiality, and that the music's sheer cleverness is too often an end in itself. "Tomorrow Never Knows" may have borrowed its central metaphysical conceit rather uncritically, but at least here the song and the sounds and effects are working toward the same end and are very much of a piece. On *Sgt. Pepper*, with one or two exceptions, the extraordinarily creative songwriting that so distinguished *Revolver* and *Rubber Soul* is in critically short supply.

The Beatles created their psychedelic rock entirely in the studio, without having to worry about how and whether the new sounds might translate in concert. In San Francisco, the situation was very different. The Grateful Dead, the Jefferson Airplane, Big Brother and the Holding Company (with Janis Joplin), and most of the other San Francisco bands had developed along with an audience that largely shared their backgrounds, their values, and their choice of chemical stimulation. They played both for and with the dancers, and their song arrangements expanded (or exploded) according to the evolving dynamic of the city's unique dance-concerts, which took place weekly in old ballrooms like the Avalon and Fillmore, and frequent free concerts in the parks. Many of the musicians had been coffeehouse folkies and were not well prepared for the demands of extended improvisation. But the nurturing Bay Area ambience gave them room to grow and learn; the audiences neither expected nor valued flash and polish and were willing to forgive stumbling

and wrong turns as long as they were *going somewhere*. The light shows, poster art, and underground comics that flourished along with the rock bands also relied on the local milieu for inspiration and support. This was a kind of rock and roll renaissance, remarkably free of commercial constraints and pressures. The corporate record labels ignored it for a while, but inevitably they descended on the scene like robber barons, signing up all the popular bands, beginning with the Jefferson Airplane.

Most of these bands were so thoroughly oriented toward live performance that they did not immediately feel at home in the recording studio. On tape, limitations that hadn't mattered in the dance halls—sloppy ensembles, directionless jamming, the difference between improvising off the energy of the dancers and the moment and improvising solos that would stand up musically to repeated listening—were glaringly evident. The Grateful Dead's first album was a stiff, ramshackle affair, but they had wisely negotiated a contract that allowed them practically unlimited studio time and soon got down to work learning to use the technology for their own ends. Jefferson Airplane, a band with perhaps too many ex-folkie troubadors for its own good, at least had recourse to a diverse songwriting output, plus an accomplished and inventive jazz-stoked rhythm section. Big Brother and the Holding Company were in many ways a punk band before their time— rough, ragged, loud, and snotty, specialists in garage-band mayhem. The media soon singled out their vocalist, Janis Joplin, for praise, with predictable results: band splits, chanteuse goes out on her own. As has often been the case throughout rock's history, several of the less-hyped "second tier" San Francisco bands have proved especially influential among subsequent generations of rockers: Santana, Quicksilver Messenger Service, Moby Grape.

In Los Angeles, Beach Boy Brian Wilson responded to the Beatles' challenge with his own acid-drenched studio creations: *Pet Sounds* and the sonically devastating "Good Vibrations." If the Byrds failed to follow up on the promise of mid-sixties masterworks like "Eight Miles High," "Why," and "5D (Fifth Dimension)," opting to return to their folk and country roots, L.A. bands such as Love, the Doors, Clear Light, and Kaleidoscope remained committed to their own versions of "the quest." In London, an underground flourished briefly around the UFO Club, where the reigning masters of psychedelic weirdness were unquestionably Pink Floyd. Like the San Francisco bands, the Floyd, Soft Machine, and their fellow travelers originally developed their music in conjunction with an audience of tripsters, as a kind of underground alternative to the pop-music bandwagon. But the honeymoon would be even briefer than in San Francisco.

"The first night of UFO was December 23, 1966," recalls record producer Joe Boyd, an American who had arrived in Britain in 1965 to open a London office for Elektra records (U.S. home label for the Butterfield Blues Band, the Doors, and Love, among others). "And in three months the club went from being nonexistent to being the club that defined which groups were hot, which groups would go down well on the university concert circuit; by spring 1967, Pink Floyd was already on the record charts. For maybe eight to ten months in all there was a real underground scene, coming out of the art schools for the most part, with venues that weren't normal venues, an audience that wasn't a normal audience, and light shows, which were not a normal part of presenting groups. And it took less than a year for it to become part of the mainstream of the pop-music industry."

A number of bands that began in the heady period of 1968–1970 continued to make highly experimental music. In Britain, Hawkwind chased the psychedelic dragon's tail through years of personnel changes and individual and collective ups and downs. They even survived the defection of their personable, gruff-voiced singer-bassist Lemmy, who subsequently formed pioneering thrash-metal band Motorhead with the idea of creating a sound so brutal it would wither your lawn. In Germany, Can, Faust, and Neu grounded their sonic experimentation in the modular repetition-structures employed by La Monte Young, Terry Riley, and other avant-garde minimalists, taking their cues from the first rock band to incorporate these influences successfully, New York's Velvet Underground.

But in most art forms, periods of feverish experimentation inevitably give way to periods of reflection and retrenchment; what goes up must come down. The spate of drug-related deaths that decimated rock's ranks during the late sixties was bound to have a sobering effect. And in their search for musical values that would provide some solid grounding in the trip's inevitable aftermath, many musicians turned to the sustaining verities of the tradition, to their folk and country roots. The Byrds' *Sweetheart of the Rodeo* (with the star-crossed country-rock innovator Gram Parsons) and Dylan's *John Wesley Harding* (both from 1968) set the tone for this back-to-the-roots movement. Equally crucial were the first two albums by Dylan's former backing group, the Band (née Hawks). *Music From Big Pink* (1968) and *The Band* (1969) were steeped in Americana, sounding superficially like the aural equivalent of a nineteenth-century tintype. A closer listen revealed a group that was experimental as well as firmly rooted; the "little black boxes" that guitarist Robbie Robertson and organist Garth Hudson fed their signals through were hardly traditional instrumentation, and what sounded like a rustic jew's harp turned out to be an electric keyboard instrument, a clavinet, played through a wah-wah pedal. Even the Grateful Dead returned to their roots in folk, country, bluegrass, and jug-band music in 1970 for two of their most consistently rewarding albums, *Workingman's Dead* and *American Beauty*. Once country rock reared its head, the neo-folkie harmonies of Crosby, Stills, and Nash and the early-seventies proliferation of introspective, folk-based singer-songwriters were sure to follow. The Eagles were just around the bend.

For all its brevity and evanescence, the "quest for pure sanity" in sound has left a surprisingly rich and lasting legacy. The recording-studio experimentation that flourished during this period, fueled by the healthy competition between bands and artists from Los Angeles and San Francisco to London and Berlin, is one aspect of this legacy. Another is the freedom that rock musicians won to explore these experiments without undue commercial and record-company pressures—freedom that was in many cases hard-won, and which, like most freedoms, has had to be fought for again and again.

The *musical* impact of psychedelia has been pervasive, not just in progressive or album rock but in idioms as different as funk (Sly and the Family Stone, George Clinton and Parliament-Funkadelic) and contemporary electronic dance music of the trance, ambient, and acid house persuasions. It's true that the main lines of rock and roll's development have largely rejected psychedelia's more extended forays into formlessness. For the most part, the bands that applied their search for new sounds in the service of the song, rather than indulging in freak-outs for their own sake, have been the bands with the most lasting influence. But this is only part of the story.

"So many of the fundamental assumptions behind the way people approach making music today wouldn't be there if it hadn't been for the music of the psychedelic era," says Joe Boyd, who now runs his own highly eclectic label, Hannibal Records. "The foundation of rock and roll was always this standard guitar-bass-drums structure, which came out of rhythm and blues and jazz. What psychedelic music did was to open the music up to Indian and Arabic influences—guitar solos based on modal scales replacing chord-based improvisation, the introduction of the drone. With Pink Floyd you had a definite classical influence coming in. You had an opening up to avant-garde jazz, so you had dissonances coming in. The long-term effects have been so pervasive. I would compare it to reggae, which has been incredibly influential on pop music, so that today very few drummers or bass players are *not* influenced by the reggae way of hearing rhythms. It's become so much a part of the way everybody plays that people just don't notice it anymore, and I think the same is true of those influences from the psychedelic era. They've become so much a part of the musical landscape that they're just accepted as being part of the way music is played and recorded."

Right now, in a town or city near you, the quest for pure sanity goes on. Meanwhile, the original conspirators are still wondering whether they understand *what really happened.* "Why we got away with it I don't know," admits the Airplane's Paul Kantner. "Maybe when you're dealing with authority, you just have to go on and do what you want, and then see what you get. Sometimes the laws fall before you like cards if you just go take what you want. On the other hand, we once supposed that this was an *ongoing* CIA investigation, of introducing LSD into the culture to see how it would affect people; that they would keep us from getting arrested, just so we could continue with the experiment as they observed us from afar. And we certainly got away with everything we wanted to get away with—everything and more."

Ken Kesey echoes and amplifies these sentiments: "I don't know; it's been examined and reexamined over and over. What I do know is that this revolution in consciousness changes you at the core of your soul. And I know that we're not finished with it yet: The sixties just won't be over until the fat lady gets high. This is hard for a lot of fat ladies to acknowledge, but it's the truth."

Article 11. Robert Palmer

1. How did LSD affect the way people made music in San Francisco in the 60s?

2. Name two early and important songs that exemplify the effects of LSD on rock music, and discuss how they illustrate those effects.

3. How did the Acid Tests contribute to the development of the Grateful Dead's approach to music making?

4. What did the acid rockers learn from the jazzman John Coltrane?

5. In what way(s) did the Beatles' psychedelic music differ from that of San Francisco bands like the Grateful Dead?

6. Do you think acid rock music could have existed without LSD? That is, were drugs necessary? Would or could musicians have created the music without them?

7. Would you have wanted to be there? Why, or why not?

8. What is the legacy of acid rock?

9. Write a short essay discussing the influence of drugs on rock in two different eras.

Part

V

Censorship and Rock

Can I Play with Madness?
Mysticism, Horror, and Postmodern Politics

■■

Robert Walser

Cradled in evil, that Thrice-Great Magician,
The Devil, rocks our souls, that can't resist;
And the rich metal of our own volition
Is vaporized by that sage alchemist.
　　　　　　　　　　　　　—Baudelaire

In his course on rhetoric, the Roman orator Quintilian included a fictitious legal exercise in the politics of music and madness. He presented the case of a musician who is accused of manslaughter because he played in the wrong musical mode during a sacrifice; by playing in the Phrygian mode, a piper allegedly caused the officiating priest to go mad and fling himself over a cliff. Quintilian used this story to support his argument that musical training is essential for the development of oratorical skills, but the problem of the musician's liability is also of interest because it raises questions about the nature and power of music, about social mistrust of those whose rhetorical abilities find their outlet through musical discourse. As the popularity of heavy metal grew in the late 1980s, it came increasingly under fire from critics who accused its musicians of "playing in the wrong mode," causing madness and death. In this chapter I will criticize a number of influential condemnations of heavy metal and propose alternative explanations of the significance of mysticism, horror, and violence in heavy metal.

Professing Censorship: The PMRC and its Academic Allies Attack

The single most influential critic of heavy metal in the 1980s was Tipper Gore, whose status as the wife of U.S. Senator Albert Gore, Jr., provided her with access to media attention and political muscle to support her cause. In 1985, Gore, along with several other wives of powerful government figures (among them Susan Baker, wife of then treasury secretary James A. Baker) established the Parents' Music Resource Center (PMRC). The PMRC has been quite successful in articulating a reactionary cultural agenda and accomplishing its political goals. Since its founding, the group has pressured record companies into placing warning stickers on recordings with "adult" lyrics and has underwritten partially successful campaigns to persuade state legislatures to censor certain types of music, chiefly rap and heavy metal. Through its conjugal connections with Capitol Hill, the PMRC was able to provoke congressional hearings, in September 1985, on the subject of what they called "porn rock." Though the PMRC and Congress described the hearings as neutral "fact-finding," others saw them as terrorism, since congressional interrogation of musicians and leaders of the music industry suggested implicit (and illegal) threats of legislation if the moralistic demands of the PMRC for "voluntary" censorship were not met.

Although the PMRC has been accused of not really being a "resource center" because its publications display little familiarity with the scholarly literature on popular music, it is unmistakably "parental." The fullest articulation of the PMRC brief is Tipper Gore's *Raising PG Kids in an X-Rated Society*, published in 1987. In it, Gore takes care to establish her authority as a social and cultural critic by emphasizing that she is a parent; she dwells on the numbers and genders of the children of PMRC leaders, while neglecting to mention that her main opponents at the Senate hearings, musicians Frank Zappa and Dee Snider, are also concerned parents. Her references to twenty-year-old "boys" mark her concern to represent heavy metal as a threat to youth, enabling her to mobilize parental hysteria while avoiding the adult word *censorship*. Objecting to eroticism and "lesbian undertones" in popular music, along with sadism and brutality, she conflates sex and violence, which have in common their threat to parental control.

It is clear from Gore's book that heavy metal participates in a crisis in the reproduction of values, that it is a threat because it celebrates and legitimates sources of identity and community that do not derive from parental models. For the PMRC, assuming the universality of "the American Family," an institution of mythic stature but scant abundance, provides an absolute norm that can be righteously defended. Gore attempts to naturalize her perspective by appealing to "common sense" universals, such as the "shared moral values" that underpin "our" society. She combines such grand claims with disingenuousness about her own

political clout, as when she refers to "our friends (some of whom happen to hold public office)." Like so many recent appeals to "common sense" and "morality," Gore's book is a call for the imposition of official values and the elimination of cultural difference.

To bolster her attack on heavy metal, Gore relies heavily on a pamphlet by a professor of music, "The Heavy Metal User's Manual" by Joe Stuessy. Not only is Stuessy often cited in Gore's book; he was also called upon as an expert witness for the Senate hearings in 1985. In both his testimony and his pamphlet, Stuessy argued that heavy metal lyrics are violent and deviant and that metal music is artistically impoverished. "Most of the successful heavy metal," he testified, "projects one or more of the following basic themes: extreme rebellion, extreme violence, substance abuse, sexual promiscuity/perversion (including homosexuality, bisexuality, sadomasochism, necrophilia, etc.), Satanism." In fact, heavy metal lyrics dealing with these topics are uncommon. For example, examination of eighty-eight song lyrics reprinted by *Hit Parader* reveals relatively little concern with violence, drug use, or suicide. Reduced to the crudest terms, the songs could be grouped thematically so:

Assertion of or longing for intensity: 27
Lust: 17
Loneliness, victimization, self-pity: 17
Love: 14 (affirmation, 8; regret or longing, 6)
Anger, rebellion, madness: 8
Didactic or critical (antidrug, anti-Devil, anti-TV evangelism, critique of the subversion of justice by wealth): 5

Moreover, when such transgressive lyrics do appear, it is in contexts where they often function in ways that are more complex and sophisticated than Stuessy recognizes, as we will see below.

Connections between heavy metal and drug use have certainly existed throughout the music's history, beginning perhaps with the success of Blue Cheer among San Francisco speed freaks in the late 1960s. But drugs cannot explain a style of music, since the music, lyrics, and images of even heavily drug-influenced music cross the boundaries of subcultural scenes and make sense to people who are using different drugs or even no drugs at all. And because both music and drugs are involved in strategies for coping with particular social circumstances, criticism of one cannot depend on denunciation of the other; both must be located in the real world of material and cultural tensions. Moreover, critics have failed to notice that as heavy metal became both individually and collectively more virtuosic during the 1980s, musicians increasingly confided that they could no longer afford to indulge in drugs and alcohol because their music would suffer too much.

Finally, criticism of rock music because of drug use often implicitly relies upon an absurdly sanitized version of musical history. Many now-canonic nineteenth-century artists "confidently engaged in 'mad' behavior— debauchery, drinking, drug use, irrational thinking—hoping thus to stimulate their creativity . . . . the viewpoint prevailed that genius and madness are inseparable." Berlioz made no bones about his use of opium; his program for the *Symphonie fantastique* explicitly connects opium use with the rhetorical splendor of his music. Abuse of alcohol is well documented for composers such as Schumann, Schubert, and Mussorgsky, and much more information about drugs and canonic composers would no doubt be available were it not for the musicological whitewashing of the lives of these musicians, which has retroactively enforced compulsory sobriety, heterosexuality, and Christianity. Berlioz's *Symphonie fantastique* is, of course, more than the random outcome of an opium dream that it pretends to be; it is a powerful metaphorical articulation, grounded in contemporary social currents and musical discourses. Contemporary popular music is made to seem especially vulnerable to certain kinds of critique because so much has been purged from our hagiological histories of music and so much is hidden by the assumptions about cultural hierarchy we take for granted.

Throughout his book, Stuessy pursues the simplistic argument that healthy minds don't think negative thoughts, and he alleges that heavy metal is socially unique in its glorification of violence, which network news shows, for example, merely report. But Steussy, like Gore, is being disingenuous, because struggles for power are hardly unique to youth culture or popular culture. From the Super Bowl to Monster Truck races, from Capitol Hill to corporate boardrooms (where handbooks of advice have titles like *Swim with the Sharks* and *Leadership Secrets of Atilla the Hun*), adult Americans (especially men) display their seemingly insatiable fascination with power and violence, a way of thinking that is continually affirmed by the brutality of American capitalism and government policy. From President Johnson's War on Poverty to President Bush's War on Drugs, American politicians have found military metaphors the most effective means of selling programs that might have been described in communal and compassionate terms. In this light, Stuessy's concluding recommendations for action against metal are patently hypocritical: "I think the attack on heavy metal must be waged on all fronts using every weapon at our disposal. . . . Warning labels and ratings might be helpful, but that is not the final solution. Printed lyrics would be helpful, but that is not the ultimate weapon." Glorification of violence in American society is hardly deviant, as we see from Stuessy's own plan for a "final solution" to the problem of heavy metal.

Stuessy's status as a professor of music makes him a useful ally to those who would strip heavy metal of First Amendment protections as free artistic expression, for he is able to offer an aggressive twist on the usual mystification that elevates classical music and protects it from ideological critique, leaving popular musics more vulnerable to attack. Stuessy assures us that the process of artistic creation remains "shrouded in mystery," and the inspiration of composers like Beethoven was "mysterious and quite possibly divine"; but heavy metal, he argues, is merely cranked out according to a formula, which disqualifies it from protection under freedom of expression, making it instead subject to "consumer protection" regulation like other manufactured products.

At the same time, the aesthetic tradition has been so successful in effacing the social meanings of culture that Stuessy found it necessary to argue at length that music can in fact affect us. He adopts, and Gore accepts from him, a "hypodermic model" of musical effects;

music's meanings are "pounded" or "dumped" into listeners, who are helpless to resist. Young people in particular are thought to be more vulnerable, especially when repetitive listening and headphone use help create "a direct, unfettered freeway straight into the mind." Stuessy's problem is to define music so that heavy metal can be held responsible for harming listeners without calling into question the violence in Beethoven's *Eroica*, for example, or the glorification of drugs, violence, and Satanism in the *Symphony fantastique*. The solution is simply to assume that the meanings of classical music are essentially benign because they are art, whereas heavy metal ought to arouse our suspicions because it is popular and commercially successful. Those who embrace such a position seem undaunted by the elitism that is required to underpin it, or by the fact that what we now call "classical music" is and always has been "commercial."

Another academic, this one a professor of religious studies at the University of Denver, has recently launched a full-scale attack on heavy metal. Like several earlier book-length denunciations of rock music, Carl A. Raschke's *Painted Black: From Drug Killings to Heavy Metal—the Alarming True Story of How Satanism Is Terrorizing Our Communities* is explicitly concerned with defending "the values of Christian civilization," which he presumes are shared by all right-thinking citizens. The book "reveals" a national epidemic of Satanism, manifest in ritual crimes and supported by heavy metal music. Unlike Tipper Gore's book, which maintains a rather calm tone and clear documentation, Raschke's is a potboiler, filled with sensational claims backed by shoddy scholarship. On the one hand, he uses unsubstantiated and marginally coherent similes to suggest that heavy metal is a terrible threat: "The end result [of heavy metal] is to erode the nervous system with noise, as drugs destroy the cerebrum"; "A national epidemic of 'satanist-related' crime was growing faster than AIDS"; and, most puzzling: "Heavy metal belongs to a so-called avant-garde art form that has stayed veiled from the eyes of mass audiences, the style known as aesthetic terrorism."

On the other hand, Raschke also pretends to have objective, scientific justification for his hysteria:

> In 1985, the *Wall Street Journal* reported that a fat sheaf of neuro-psychological research has shown remarkable, and complex, relationships between music listening and brain organization. Roger Shepard, a professor at Stanford University, believes that certain kinds of music "mesh effectively with the deep cognitive structures of the mind." Heavy metal seems to mesh with the limbic brain, the most primitive and potentially violent stratum of cerebral processing.

But the last, damning sentence of this passage is a deliberate fabrication, for heavy metal was never mentioned by Shepard. Raschke has tacked onto his summary of a quite uncontroversial report his own condemnation of heavy metal, carefully couched in scientific language ("limbic brain," "cerebral processing") so as to suggest that it is justified by the findings of Shepard's research. He misleads his readers in an attempt to whip up a repressive frenzy directed against metal musicians and fans. Raschke invokes science as part of his effort to essentialize what are in fact social tensions: "Heavy metal does more than dissolve the inherent inhibitions against violence. It actively fosters, configures, anneals, reinforces, and purifies the most vicious and depraved tendencies within the human organism." When he describes both "inhibitions against violence" *and* "depraved tendencies" as inherent qualities rather than socially negotiated ones, Raschke wants to have it both ways: heavy metal dissolves the fragile bonds of repression that make civilization possible, *and* it unnaturally corrupts human nature itself.

The terrorism of Raschke and similar critics depends upon two tactics: anecdote and insinuation. Raschke himself cites a group of sociologists of religion who determined that there was "not a shred of evidence" that Satanism is a problem in America, directly contradicting the thesis of Raschke's book. The "evidence disintegrates as close examination occurs" whenever Satanism and crime are linked, according to J. Gordon Melton, director of the Institute for the Study of American Religion in Santa Barbara. Raschke replies by recounting, in sickening detail, a few instances of crimes involving satanic symbols, without addressing the question of how significant this sort of crime is—how it compares statistically with, for example, crimes committed by clergy or suicides related to plant closings. In Stuessy's book, in Raschke's, and in a lecture I heard by a touring campus crusader against rock music, I found the same handful of stories repeated rapidly and balefully so as to suggest that they stood as select examples of widespread trends rather than the bizarre and anomalous events they were. In the end Raschke waffles and hedges: "And if no one can blame rock music directly for the 300 percent rise in adolescent suicides or the 7 percent increase in teenage pregnancies, it *may surely* be more than a negligible factor." With the word *may*, Raschke admits that no link can be made; with the word *surely*, he attempts to cover up that admission. Moreover, if we assume that rock music is to blame for that rise in suicides, do we then credit rap and heavy metal with causing the dramatic decrease in drug use among high school students in the 1980s, the decade during which those styles came to dominate musical culture?

In fact, none of these critics is able to connect heavy metal directly with suicide, Satanism, or crime. Tipper Gore does provide information on Dungeons and Dragons, a fantasy role-playing game that has been attacked for the same reasons. According to her, over eight million sets of D&D have been sold in the United States; yet even the game's harshest critics can link it with fewer than fifty people involved in suicides or homicides. As with metal, one might reasonably infer from such statistics that D&D is to be applauded as a stabilizing factor in many adolescent lives. If I have dwelt on these critiques longer than seems necessary, it is because they have in fact been extremely influential. The flimsiness of these arguments seems to escape readers who are predisposed to accept heavy metal as a convenient scapegoat; Raschke was given a complimentary "Portrait," for example, in *The Chronicle of Higher Education*.

Gore and other critics also point to actual violence at heavy metal concerts as more proof of the music's malignancy. But such violence is greatly exaggerated by metal's critics; mayhem is no more common at metal concerts than at sports events—or at the opera in nineteenth-century Paris or performances of Shakespeare in nineteenth-century New York. In fact, concert security guards report that crowds at country music concerts are far more difficult to manage than heavy metal crowds. Culture is valued because it mobilizes meanings with respect to the most deeply held social values and the most profound tensions. Only by effacing cultural history can heavy metal be portrayed as singularly violent in thought or deed. But insinuations of metal's violent effects are also contradicted by a recent study that finds no correlation between teenagers' preferences in music and their likelihood of having "behavioral problems" at school.

To be sure, Tipper Gore raises legitimate concerns about sexual violence in the lyrics and visual representations of metal shows. But she labors to portray such violence as an aberration of youth and commercial exploitation, scapegoating heavy metal musicians and fans for problems that are undeniably extant but for which she holds entirely blameless the dominant social systems, institutions, and moral values she defends. Calls for censorship serve to divert attention from the real social causes of violence and misogyny.

All of these critics share the notion that heavy metal is bad because it is perverse deviance in the midst of a successfully functioning society. They ascribe much too much importance to a transhistorical notion of "adolescence," which allows them to overlook the specific forms that culture takes in particular circumstances of power and pain. They believe that insisting that "healthy minds don't think negative thoughts" will make people overlook the devastation caused by deindustrialization and disastrous social policies. They imagine that fans are passive, unable to resist the pernicious messages of heavy metal, and thus they themselves commit the sort of dehumanization they ascribe to popular culture. They make fans into dupes without agency or subjectivity, without social experiences and perceptions that might inform their interactions with mass-mediated texts. And they portray heavy metal musicians as "outside agitators," just as social authorities tried to blame civil rights violence on Communist troublemaking, as though poverty, joblessness, and police brutality weren't sufficient explanation. But heavy metal exists not in a world that would be fine if it were not marred by degraded culture, but in a world disjointed by inequity and injustice.

In his 1987 movie, *The Hidden*, director Jack Sholder satirized such portrayals of the horrific effects of heavy metal. The back of the videocassette release summarizes the plot: "a demonic extraterrestrial creature is invading the bodies of innocent victims—and transforming them into inhuman killers with an unearthly fondness for heavy metal music, red Ferraris and unspeakable violence." *The Hidden* replicates precisely the understanding of heavy metal promoted by its harshest critics, linking metal with violence, and depicting it as a threat coming from elsewhere, with no connection to this world, working its evil on helpless, innocent victims. The arguments of critics like Gore, Stuessy, and Raschke depend upon denying fans subjectivity or social agency so that they can be cast as victims who can be protected through censorship. By depicting fans as "youth," an ideological category that lifts them out of society and history, these critiques manage to avoid having to provide any explanation of why fans are attracted to the specific sounds, images, and lyrics of heavy metal.

Suicide Solutions

The most celebrated public controversy over heavy metal to date revolved around a lawsuit against Judas Priest, tried in 1990. Five years earlier, two young men from Reno, Nevada—Ray Belknap, eighteen, and Jay Vance, twenty—had consummated a suicide pact by taking turns with a shotgun. Belknap was killed instantly; Vance survived to undergo three years of reconstructive surgery before dying of a drug overdose in 1988. Both men had been avid Judas Priest fans, and the suit alleged that subliminal messages embedded in the band's 1978 release, *Stained Class*, had created a com-

pulsion that led to their deaths. According to the plaintiffs, one song contained commands of "do it" that were audible only subconsciously, and other songs, when played backward, exhorted "try suicide," "suicide is in," and "sing my evil spirit." As with previous accusations of "backward masking" in rock music, the suit depended on the premise that such hidden messages can be decoded without conscious awareness and on the idea that they affect listeners more powerfully than overt communication.

The strategy of the defense was simple: they argued that the lives of Vance and Belknap had been such that no mysterious compulsion was required to account for their suicides. During the two years preceding the suicide pact, for example, Vance had run away from home thirteen times; his mother admitted beating him "too often" when he was young. His father beat him, too, especially after he lost his job (when a GM plant closed in 1979) and began drinking heavily. Vance's violent behavior long predated his involvement with heavy metal; a school psychiatrist had expressed concern about his self-destructive behavior when Vance was in second grade, and his mother testified that he had tried to strangle her and hit her with a hammer while he was still in grade school. He had even been institutionalized for attempted suicide in 1976, at age eleven.

Ray Belknap's background was just as bad. At the time of his suicide attempt, he had just decided to quit his job with a local contractor, after his boss had won his week's wages in a pool game. His mother, a born-again Christian whose religious beliefs increased the tension at home, had just separated from her fourth husband, "a reportedly violent man who had once been arrested for menacing Ray's mother with a gun" and who sometimes locked Ray in the garage and beat him with a belt. Defense lawyers argued that in such circumstances, there was little need to postulate secret musical compulsions in order to account for suicidal thoughts. The prosecution replied that many people have bad home lives yet do not kill themselves—a risky line of reasoning, one would think, since their case depended on overlooking the millions of people who listen to heavy metal yet do not kill themselves.

The Judas Priest case hinged, though, on the question of the impact of subliminal commands, allegedly masked but made no less effective by being placed on the album backward. As part of the substantial media attention given the case, "Newsline New York" interviewed an "expert," Wilson Bryan Key, who claimed that such messages in heavy metal music lead to violence. (The host of the show neglected to mention that Key has in the past claimed to have found satanic or sexual messages on Ritz crackers, $5 bills, and Howard Johnson's placemats.) Yet studies by psychologists have repeatedly shown that while intelligible messages can be found in virtually anything played backward, there is no evidence that listeners perceive or are affected by backward messages. "Even when messages are there, all they do is add a little noise to the music," says one researcher. "There is absolutely no effect from content."

Lead singer Rob Halford may have tipped the scales of justice when he appeared for the last day of testimony with a tape containing backward messages *he* had found on the *Stained Class* album. Reversing the fragment "strategic force / they will not" from "Invader" yielded an intelligible, if cryptic, "It's so fishy, personally I'll owe it." Halford reversed "They won't take our love away," from the same song, and had the courtroom howling when they heard "Hey look, Ma, my chair's broken." Finally, he played his last discovery: "Stand by for exciter/Salvation is his task" came out backward as "I-I-I as-asked her for a peppermint-t-t / I-I-I asked for her to get one."

The trial ended with Judas Priest cleared of all charges, for the judge remained unconvinced that the "subliminal" messages on the album were intentionally placed there or were necessary to explain the conduct of Vance and Belknap. There seemed no credible motive for the subliminal crimes of which the band was accused; as their lawyer put it, "In order to find for the plaintiffs here, you'd have to assume that there is at work out there an Evil Empire of the media and the artist who want to damage the people who are buying their works. You hafta be nuts to think that if Judas Priest had the capability to insert a subliminal

message they would tell the fans who've been buying all their albums, 'Go kill yourselves.'"

In the face of such evidence, why is it that accusations of subliminal compulsions persist? Those who condemn heavy metal often posit conspiracies in order to scapegoat musicians and fans, avoiding questions of social responsibility for the destructive behavior of people such as Vance and Belknap. But charges of secret messages may persist because we as a society have afforded ourselves no other ways of explaining music's power to affect us. Subliminal manipulation substitutes for a conception of music as a social discourse; since we are trained not to think of music, or any other art, as symbolic discourse, drawing its power from socially grounded desires and contestations, we fall back on a kind of mysticism to explain the effects that music undeniably produces. Such effects may be acceptable when they are created by dead "great" composers, but they are perceived as dangerously manipulative when produced by others, such as heavy metal musicians.

Another reason the Priest suit hinged on subliminal messages was that an important precedent had already been set in 1985, when a judge decided that overt lyrics about suicide were protected speech under the First Amendment. This earlier case was a suit against Ozzy Osbourne, whose song "Suicide Solution" (1981) was alleged to have promoted suicide in its lyrics and to have compelled nineteen-year-old John McCullom to shoot himself. Osbourne's claim that the lyrics were inspired by the alchohol-related suicide of a friend and that the song is in fact antisuicide and antidrug in sentiment was dismissed as sham social conscience, feigned after the fact. Although this suit too was eventually dismissed, the case became a cause célèbre, for it was timely. The PMRC was in the midst of a campaign against Osbourne and other musicians that had just culminated in widespread discussion of regulation of the record industry and the infamous Senate hearings, and they were quick to use the McCullom suicide as yet another example of the evil effects of heavy metal.

But despite his reputation for transgression—he once bit the head off a live bat (which he thought was rubber) tossed onstage by a fan—Ozzy Osbourne's lyrics tend to be quite moralistic. His *Blizzard of Ozz* album (1981), which contains "Suicide Solution," also includes an antiporn song, "No Bone Movies," which deplores the degradation caused by obsessive lust. "Revelation (Mother Earth)" is a plea for environmental responsibility, and "Crazy Train" attributes its craziness to the modern pressures faced by the "heirs of a cold war." "Steal Away (The Night)" celebrates love; "Goodbye to Romance" mourns its loss. And in "Mr. Crowley," Osbourne's lyrics refer to the infamous English Satanist Aleister Crowley (1875–1947); but far from celebrating occult practices, the song taunts Crowley, displaying an ironic tone often used by Osbourne (and never noticed by his literal-minded critics). Osbourne evokes the fascination with the supernatural that Crowley represents—"Uncovering things that were sacred/manifest on this earth"—at the same time that he tweaks Crowley's nose:

Mister Charming, did you think you were pure?
Mister Alarming, in nocturnal rapport

Mister Crowley, won't you ride my white horse?
Mister Crowley, it's symbolic, of course.

Osbourne plays with signs of the supernatural because they evoke a power and mystery that is highly attractive to many fans, but his song offers an experience of those qualities and even a critique, not a literal endorsement of magical practices.

Suicide is a serious problem (some estimates report six thousand teenage suicides per year in the United States), and that is why popular artists address it. But music does not simply inflict its meanings upon helpless fans; texts become popular when people find them meaningful in the contexts of their own lives. That is why a wide range of responses is possible; indeed, the evidence suggests that only a tiny minority of fans found "Suicide Solution" depressing rather than sobering and thought-provoking. One fan wrote to Metallica to thank them because he had decided *not* to kill himself after hearing their song about suicide, "Fade to Black." The lead singer of Dark Angel described a song from their album *Leave Scars* (1989): "There's a song called 'The Promise of Agony' that covers the depression and anxiety of being an adolescent. Hopefully there will be kids who pick up the new album and realize from reading the lyrics that even in their darkest despair they really aren't alone."

A study of patients hospitalized for contemplating suicide indicates that a feeling of helplessness is the strongest predictor of which of them would actually go on to kill themselves. Nobody listens to heavy metal because it makes them feel helpless. Sociologists distinguish between fatalistic suicide, caused by overregulation, and anomic suicide, attributable to nonintegration. Donna Gaines points out that many young people are doubly vulnerable, since they feel both overregulated by adults and alienated from them. It is possible that texts can resonate with such attitudes; Goethe's *The Sorrows of Young Werther* seems to have helped make suicide a Continental fad of the late 1770s. But although its explicit treatments of violence might make suicide seem more familiar, metal is attractive precisely because it offers a way of overcoming those feelings of loneliness and helplessness. Even when it models musical despair, heavy metal confronts issues that cannot simply be dismissed or repressed, and it positions listeners as members of a community of fans, making them feel that they belong to a group that does not regulate them.

The vast majority of heavy metal fans don't worship Satan and don't commit suicide; yet many fans enjoy that fraction of heavy metal songs that deals with such things. Heavy metal's critics have provided no credible explanations for this, for they deny fans the agency that is necessary for attraction to exist, preferring to believe that such images are inflicted rather than sought. To find this unsatisfactory is to open up the problem of explaining the attractiveness of mysticism and horror.

Article 12. Robert Walser

1. How did the ideas and goals of the PMRC reflect the contemporaneous political situation in America?

2. What exactly was the PMRC reacting to in heavy metal music?

3. According to the "hypodermic model" of musical effects, music "inflicts" its meanings upon helpless fans. Are listeners truly unthinking dupes, unable to interpret what they hear or see? Are you?

4. Why can't drug use "explain" heavy metal?

5. What is "backward masking"?

6. What is censorship?

7. According to Walser, why does the idea of subliminal compulsion (through such things as backward masking) persist?

8. To what extent do the themes heard in heavy metal reflect our society?

9. Discuss a famous case of censorship and popular music in the 90s.

Part

VI

Women in Rock

Girl Groups:
A Ballad of Codependency

Donna Gaines

Hey Jawn-ny, wuh coluh are huh eyes?
I dunno, she's oh-ways wearin' shades.
Yo, is she tawwwl?
Well, I gotta look up.

I had forgotten about the Shangri-Las until that night. I was standing at the foot of the stage in a drunken haze, late 1970s at some downtown New York City hole like the old Ritz or the Peppermint Lounge. The Heartbreakers were careening through another fuck-brilliant set. There stood the immortal Johnny Thunders, ex-New York Doll, cranking his lead, with Walter Lure on rhythm, bantering back and forth, in deep-Queens dialect.

The Dolls had genderfucked their cover of the Shangri-Las' "Give Him a Great Big Kiss" too, paying homage to a group of glorious hitter chicks from Cambria Heights, Queens. Actually, with the grease and glamour hairdos, all douched up in frilly blouses, what were the New York Dolls anyway but a hard-rock girl-group tribute band? New York City punk-glam fashion had appropriated a fair share of post-Elvis, pre-Beatles regalia: black leather motorcycle jackets, scruffy engineer boots, tight black twill jeans, dark runny fishnets, spike heels, hair teased and sprayed, and white gooey slut lipstick. I was home.

"When I say I'm in love, you best believe I'm in love, L-U-V!"

While the Ronettes had the hotter look—bigger hair, heavier eyeliner, tighter clothes—the Shangri-Las were bolder. Their songs were portraits of tough girls, street queens as fearless as the wild boys they worshiped. Known as the "bad-girl" groups, the Ronettes and Shangri-Las were my heroes.

I'm gonna walk right up to him, give him a great big kiss, Um-Wha!
Tell him that I love him, tell him that I care, tell him that I'll always be there.
—"Give Him a Great Big Kiss," The Shangri-Las

The Shangri-Las' good-bad wild boy is a rebel, a rocker who walks to the beat, singing a tune. A prize only she's hip enough to recognize and strong enough to handle. "Dirty fingernails . . . tight leather pants, high button shoes, he's always looking like he's got the blues." He's ultracool, but he *needs* her too.

The girl groups of the early 1960s ruled the airwaves around the time I hit puberty. I grew up in Rockaway Beach, Queens, a surf town later made famous by the Ramones. Although I collected many girl-group singles from 1958 to 1965, it was the Chantels, Ronettes, Shangri-Las, and Crystals who provided the soundtrack to my formative years.

The girl-group sound is atmospheric, sweet, melodramatic. This is *old school,* from the days when True Love saved your life and breaking up was the apocalypse. To the contemporary ear, the girl-group sound is sickly sweet, like the gushy center of your jelly donut the moment it explodes in your mouth. The only guys who like this stuff are sick, romantic, bubblegum fiends like the Ramones, and guys like Johnny Thunders who had an older sister hanging around the turntable.

Like the Shangri-Las and the Ronettes, the Dolls and the Ramones came from the boroughs of New York City. Intuitively, they understood the dialectic of vulnerability and guts and packed it into a perfect three-minute single. In 1974, the man who wrote and produced many of the Shangri-Las' songs, George "Shadow" Morton, produced the Dolls' second album, *Too Much Too Soon.* In 1980, Phil Spector, who discovered the Ronettes, produced the Ramones' luscious *End of the Century.* If you study Thunders's early hair, it's pure Ronnie Spector. And Joey Ramone, who sounds like Ronnie, looks a lot like Shangri-Las singer Mary Weiss (the nose, lips). These bands are New York's finest. (At this writing, Joey Ramone and Ronnie Spector are collaborating on an album.)

Social Relations

Unlike latter-day all-female bands like the Runaways or the Go-Go's, girl groups rarely wrote their own material and they never played instruments. In studio sessions and on the road, producers and managers rotated artists and backup singers as needed. Even though over a thousand girl-group records came out, most of the singers faded away from the cultural landscape except for Darlene Love and those who had hooked up with the boss—like the Ronettes' Ronnie Bennett or the Supremes' Diana Ross, to Phil Spector and Berry Gordy respectively.

Male teen idols—Fabian, Bobby Rydell, and Frankie Avalon—emerged from the teen netherworld to become centerfold icons, but girl groups were never profiled in the teen mags, even though they appeared on television shows such as *Shindig* and *Upbeat.* If they showed up in films, they performed a song or two, but the girls never appeared as actors. Instead, they got a brief taste of the high life—fancy clothes, fine dining, shiny limos, tons of fan mail, and touring with the Brit boys. It was a nice party, short-lived.

Mostly black, mainly prole teenagers, the girl groups came from the New York metropolitan area—the five boroughs of New York City, plus Long Island and New Jersey. And like their Detroit counterparts the Supremes, Martha and the Vandellas, and the Marvelettes, these girls loved to sing, often with family members—sisters, cousins, best friends.

Throughout the 1950s, boys-only doo-wop ensembles harmonized in stairwells or neighborhood store-front alcoves, after hours across the boroughs. Inspired, the girls started singing too. This was youth-generated street entertainment, as important as cruising, glue sniffing, or graffiti. It was part of early 1960s pop culture like Brooklyn's Fox Theater concerts and the Alan Freed, Murray the K, and Cousin Brucie radio shows. Some groups, such as the Shangri-Las and Chantels, also performed at local school dances. Most of the girls were still in high school, living with their parents, apparently harboring few aspirations beyond marriage and family.

Out of this, one man built an empire. Phil Spector started writing and producing songs when he was seventeen, and by the age of twenty-one he was a millionaire, the "teenage tycoon." He developed the Ronettes, Crystals, Righteous Brothers, and Darlene Love, with his signature "wall of sound." By age twenty-three Spector had eight hit singles to his credit. He called this sound "pop blues," not rock & roll.

Spector did everything—wrote or cowrote lyrics, composed music, located talent, and set up deals.

Once invented, organized, and packaged as a distinctive genre, the girl-group sound soared up the pop charts of AM radio, often bumping doo-wop, the Righteous Brothers, and the Beach Boys. From the early to mid-sixties, the girl groups were the principal women in rock.

Like most women in music (and as with black artists, generally), the girl groups' story is a typical one of under-recognition, exploitation, and disappointment. These days, when they aren't blamed for perpetrating oppressive gender ideology or mistaken for contemporary women's bands such as L7 and Babes in Toyland, the girl groups are pitied for the foul social relations that left most of them penniless and washed up by the age of twenty-one. Produced by people who specifically geared the songs to a teen market, few of these entertainers enjoyed significant careers past 1965, when surf music, the British Invasion, and Motown took the market. The Beatles and the Stones had been girl-group fans too, the boys from Liverpool covering a number of girl-group songs such as the Cookies' *Chains*, the Marvelettes' *Please Mr. Postman*, and *Baby It's You* by the Shirelles. The Stones even toured with the Ronettes but were forbidden by Spector to talk to the girls.

One critic has described the "wall of sound" as including an "R&B-derived rhythm section, generous echo and prominent choruses blending percussion, strings, saxophones, and human voices." But, in my early adolescence, the Matron Saints of Big Hair spoke to me only from the heart. Listening to it, lovesick, with a particular boy in mind, the soft strings form crescendos of tears, a much-needed catharsis for teenage heartbreak. Then bells, chimes, and a bouquet of devotional harmonies celebrate young love, human dignity reclaimed. Your best friend might get tired of hearing you obsess over "him"; the girl groups just encouraged more.

Still, after over thirty years, after Woodstock, punk, hardcore, and heavy metal, the girl groups reside at the core of my feminine identity. They've helped make me the woman I am. Not only was the sound emotionally raw, honest, and inspiring, it completely reflected my own life experience as a hitter chick coming of age in suburban Queens. It didn't matter if people thought the music was a total market fabrication, or if the most moving lyrics were written by men for girls to sing, or if the whole thing was just false consciousness. I hit puberty at the tail end of grease, when post-fifties street gangs, back-alley abortions, reform school, bad reputations, and juvenile delinquency ruled the day; when girls still had to wear skirts to public high schools and smoking cigarettes made you "tough." But I did just fine. I had the girl groups to guide the way.

Da Doo Ron Ron Run, Da Doo Ron Ron

Like punk, rap, hardcore, and death metal, girl-group music was created by teenagers for teenagers about teenage themes. But girl groups were devoted to the things teenage *girls* cared about—parental control, boys, reputations, and marriage. These were my concerns and I heard them articulated every night, under my pillow, on a transistor AM radio.

By 1964 I'd had it with the culture of domestic life. I took my pocket knife and demolished my brown-gum-soled orthopedic shoes, poured a bottle of straight hydrogen peroxide over my hair and then teased it into a high orange bouffant. I socked on wads of black eyeliner and green shadow and light-pink frosted lipstick, with thick base and face powder to cover my zits. I tweezed my eyebrows to a fine line. I traded in frumpy pleated skirts and modest pastel-colored yeshiva blouses for a new after-school look: skin-tight turquoise-blue elastic pants, slinky floral-pattern shell tops, and black pointy ankle boots with taps on the heels. Newly teenaged, I started hanging out at the subway station, at Rockaway Playland, our famous candy stores, and critical street corners across the Rockaway peninsula—wherever something was happening.

Early on, a favorite haunt was the school yard of St. Francis de Sales, in Rockaway Beach. I befriended some girls there and we spent hours watching the tall, wiry Irish-Catholic boys play basketball. For a Jewish girl like me, this was transgressive, forbidden fruit. In my neighborhood, it was a bad move—I would be presumed sexually active, wild, and dangerous.

Since I didn't have any older sisters and my older cousins were sheltered "good girls" sequestered by their parents in their bedrooms, it was the girl groups who taught me all about love, the fine art of hanging out, cosmetology, and how to guard my turf (boyfriend). My mentors also instructed me in the rudiments of class struggle, gender politics, and intergenerational conflict. The constituent elements of true love involve absolute faith, unwavering devotion, and a relentless capacity to hang in there for him, even if he treats you like shit.

Maybe

Ma-ay-be, if I pray every night, you'll come back to me.
And ma-ay-be, if I cry every day you'll come back to stay.
—"Maybe," The Chantels

The girl-group sound was ushered into U.S. cultural history in 1958 with "Maybe," the Chantels' "chick doo-wop" breakthrough hit. Some of the girl groups were fans of Frankie Lymon, with his crystal-clear falsetto voice. Unfortunately, most of the girls couldn't really sing. They had shrill voices, articulating with what I'd call a "squelp," a combination squeal and yelp. But it worked; it sounded like a real teenage girl declaring her love, demanding his. Defiant, she stood her ground against hostile forces: the town, the neighbors, parents, rival girls. It's tough talk, visceral and raw. You know it when you hear it. It's authentic to the ear, true-blue, even if nothing else about this music was. Despite the way it was written, produced, packaged, or promoted, the squelp spoke social truth.

The Chantels' Arlene Smith was not a squelper. Smith was classically trained with a rich, disciplined voice like no other. At age twelve she had performed as a soloist at Carnegie Hall. The Chantels were five friends who sang in the choir at St. Anthony of Padua in the Bronx. In time, these gospel roots translated into the celestial rhapsody of girl-group music.

"Maybe" was written by the Valentines' Richard Barrett as a powerful story of losing

someone you adore and the despair of trying to win them back. In Arlene Smith's hands, the song sounds more like she's mourning a lapse in faith. Smith was sixteen when she recorded "Maybe." She once commented that what inspired her singing in "Maybe" was the love she felt *for her parents.* Even though the lyrics spoke to heterosexual love, there's a sacredness, a fierce passion for some higher state of grace that elevates the song. This was true of a lot of the girl groups' material. "Maybe" transcended human love—she sounds like she's singing about G-d. She transports us to higher ground.

This was also characteristic of doo-wop— this cherishing and striving for redemption in love. Actually, when it comes to the torment of love, the masochism and pining away, the girl groups weren't any more soppy or sentimental than the boys. Forget Judas Priest, Ozzy, and all the other metal bands crucified for their lyrics during the PMRC-inspired witch trials of the 1980s. Doo-wop is the biggest suicide music of them all!

Gender Relations

Some songs make us morbid, but others are more famous for offending the feminist sensibility. The Rolling Stones' "Under My Thumb" and the Crystals' "He Hit Me (and It Felt Like a Kiss)" are two examples. ("He Hit Me" was written by Carole King with her husband Gerry Goffin.) But the latter song didn't exactly reflect the norms of the day—even in 1962 teachers didn't want the kids listening to it. Crystals' lead singer Barbara Alston didn't like it either, and Goffin himself admitted it was extreme for its time.

He couldn't stand to hear me say that I'd been with someone new.
And when I told him I had been untrue he hit me and it felt like a kiss.
—"He Hit Me (and It Felt Like a Kiss)," The Crystals

More than thirty years later, Hole's Courtney Love appropriated the song for a performance on *MTV Unplugged,* where she introduced it as a "really sick song." "He Hit Me" walks the line between generic sadomasochism and sheer male brutality. The protagonist cheats on her boyfriend, he gets really pissed off, he hits her, and *then* she realizes he loves her. The violence against her becomes a sign of passion, hence real caring. She is overjoyed by this act of possession, climaxing, "He made me his." Given spousal abuse rates today, there is some satisfaction in seeing guitar-slamming Courtney cover this tune. She takes it seriously, addressing an age-old nasty logic: "If he beats me, it means he loves me." She could have camped it up, or milked it for irony, but she doesn't, instead leaving it unresolved and murky, and as menacing as when the Crystals sang it.

That we can love someone even when he doesn't love us, even when he hits us, is part of the blind faith that makes this music at once so compelling and so repulsive. For example, Reparata and the Delrons' "Tommy":

> He's not so sweet and he's far from polite, hardly ever calls me, and comes to pick me up late every night,
> He's not the same boy I knew back when, but I love Tommy more than I did then.
> —"Tommy," Reparata and the Delrons

Tommy once treated our girl with consideration, respect, and tenderness. Now, for some reason she never quite raises, he starts acting like a dick. But she doesn't give up on him. Her response to his sullen indifference is to love him more!

Many of these songs portray women as submissive, needy, pining away. Yet it would be a mistake to read girl groups' music as anthems for Future Battered Wives of America. It may be true that the girls who grew up embracing these ideologies have been rewarded with a decaying suburbia, high divorce rates, and kids who worship Satan. But we can't take this music out of its historical and social context—the guys who were raised on this stuff (and boy-group doo-wop) got burned too—Vietnam, disinvestment, and bad American cars. Proving only that blind faith can kill you if you let it.

Class War

The centerpiece of both doo-wop and girl-group music is a heterosexual love that is stron-

ger than death. But with the girl groups, class antagonisms begin to surface. Not only is she expected to love him even when he beats her and ignores her, she has another function: Only a woman can offer a love that is strong enough to buffer her man against the brutalities of the workplace. In the worldview of the Crystals' "Uptown" (written by Barry Mann and Cynthia Weil), life sucks. It's degrading and cruel, except when he goes home, uptown, to her. The world he navigates is humiliating, unbearable:

> And when I take his hand, there's no man who could put him down.
> The world is sweet, it's at his feet when he's uptown.
> —"Uptown," The Crystals

Like her sisters in country, she's gotta stand by him. True love heals all wounds, including those inflicted by exploitative labor relations. The brutalities of her workplace aren't considered because, in 1962, we were all expected to marry and have babies, which, of course, wasn't acknowledged as work—they were nonalienated labors of love, L-U-V.

Despite his degraded status in the marketplace she will love him unconditionally. If he's a wild boy, unemployable and out of control, he needs her love even more. His oppositional posture offers her an advantage of reflected glory. By loving the forbidden, she gets something for herself. In 1962 adult fear and respect were hard to come by, especially for teenage girls.

> Well just because he doesn't do what everybody else does
> That's no reason why I can't give him all my love.
> —"He's a Rebel," The Crystals

Intergenerational Politics

If the role of the girl in girl groups is to be a wall of roses between her man and his world, he empowers her to resist the parents who ground her, the town that judges her harshly, the friends who shun her, the world that renders her isolated, invisible, and ineffectual. Her sins of passion and devotion cost her in the community, but they are sanctified for his name's sake.

The Shangri-Las were the most dramatic and uncompromising on these themes. In video footage, most girl group singers smile sweetly as they rant, rave, and wail against the forces of domination in their lives, contradicting the bite of the lyrics. But not Mary Weiss. She has nothing to smile about, singing about tormented boys and the price girls pay who fall in love with them. She can't fake it, not even for TV.

Over time, "Leader of the Pack" was treated as a high-cheese teen melodrama, a joke—remember "Leader of the Laundromat"? But there was risk-taking involved in loving the boy from the wrong side of town. Jimmy, Bobby, or Tommy running wild and free, scaring adults, could ruin a teenage girl's chance at a good life. He could cost her her respectability, and the relationship could tarnish the class aspirations of an entire community. In the end, the girl in the song must choose between him and her parents, between middle-class security and the road. Invariably in these songs, a tragedy occurs before she has to make a choice.

In "Leader of the Pack" her parents make it clear: She has to break up with him. When she does, he turns and walks away, and says nothing. He cracks up his bike and dies. She'll never forget him, the leader of the pack. And there she is, at the high school with all the girls in awe, asking her if she's wearing his ring, if it's great riding with him, is he picking her up after school. "Uh-Uh."

A Ballad of Codependency

It was a Friday night in the fall of 1965. I was busy getting my look together, thinking about Bobby, wondering how I could hook up with him. He'd be at Brian O'Connor's party. Brian was the leader of a loosely organized street gang that called themselves the Wizards. But the older girls said Bobby was the toughest, a little crazy if he got mad. He was seventeen, I was fourteen. At the party, the girls set it up. Janet and Linda were Jewish girls like me, who defied the norms of two very hostile communities and crossed the religion line. They looked out for me; they were sixteen and you'd best believe they could kick your ass.

I sat on Bobby's lap, we drank beers all night and made out. He was shy, he didn't say much, just smoked his Lucky Strikes. With his

pale complexion and black hair slicked back, he was cold looking, reptilian. Tall and lean, with gray horn-rimmed glasses like Buddy Holly's, in his black twill Levi's, sandy-colored desert boots, navy sport jacket, and white button-down shirt, he was *dressed.*

It got late, Bobby passed out. Brian suggested he get some air. "Bobby, why not walk Donna home?" Half conscious, he stumbled down my block and into my house—and met my parents. In my neighborhood or his, Jewish girls who dated Irish-Catholic boys were whores (pronounced "who-uhs"). My parents were different. Mom had been in show biz, and she was oblivious to the petty status hierarchies of a town where most mothers had been boring schoolteachers prior to marriage. Still, my high street visibility caused trouble, so the neighbors stepped in to control the situation. They wouldn't let their daughters hang around with me. Relatives tried to have me put away. Mom just made fun of them.

That night my parents offered Bobby a soda, but he ran for his life. Being around parents has always creeped out teenagers, especially alone in a neighborhood that's not your own, drunk on a first "date." Bobby called me up the next day, terse and to the point. "Why don't you meet me down the beach? I'll get a six-pack, Brian and the guys will be there. . . ." One-hundred-twenty-ninth Street was tough terrain, but it was his turf and I'd be totally safe with him. He was the de facto leader of the pack. But I was afraid to go because I was Jewish and it was understood that Catholic boys thought Jewish girls were "easy." (Jewish boys thought Catholic girls were whores too, but they rarely crossed over.)

I didn't go because I couldn't believe that Bobby really cared about me. I assumed he just wanted me for sex—I was a virgin. But I loved him! True love had come down while we were on the phone. He was trying to talk to me. I could hear his mother in the background yelling at him to get off the phone. He screamed back at her, "Fuck you!" and then the phone went dead. This was the first time I had ever heard anybody, male or female, curse their parents. I thought Bobby was the Duke of Earl.

Still, I never went to meet him. I never saw him again, though I carved his initials on my arm the night I stood him up. A few weeks later the older girls told me I'd really hurt him. He thought I was just using him at the party to get Brian O'Connor jealous. He had actually really cared about me. I told them I loved Bobby, not Brian, but it was too late. Bobby had gotten arrested for beating up some Jewish boys in my neighborhood. At first this episode pleased me—these guys were snobs who wouldn't talk to girls like me—but this had nothing to do with me. It was class war, ethnic cleansing in the Rockaways, something the boys played out among themselves. The girls never fought over anything except the boys. Our vendettas transcended any ethnic or religious ties.

Bobby's family was poor, they lived over the Chinese take-out in the "bad" part of Rockaway Beach. He had no dad, just a bunch of older brothers who beat the shit out of him and his younger brother. The boys Bobby pummeled lived in Neponset, the best section of the Rockaways, in big houses with loving parents. They went to prep schools and attended parent-supervised parties where they played cards. They dated obedient girls in "collegiate" garb—penny loafers, knee socks, circle pins, sweater sets, no makeup. They all went on to college where some of them smoked pot and began to question the order of things. Bobby's life followed a different story line.

Bobby was sent up to teen jail in upstate New York for beating up those guys. When he hit eighteen the judge offered to cut his sentence if he enlisted. He went to Vietnam and came out on a full psycho disability. A few years after that, he shot somebody on the street, and he's spent the rest of his life in a psychiatric prison.

Thirty years later I still hang out on the streets, but now I'm Dr. Gaines and I call it sociology. Years after the girl groups, after feminism, after everything, I still think about Bobby. I wonder how he is, rotting away somewhere, a wasted life, detached from all reality. I still believe if I had met him at the beach that day, if he had known how much I respected him, that I loved him, he might not have been so angry. Maybe he wouldn't have beaten up those guys, gone to jail and then to Vietnam. Maybe he would've seen life differently. *Maybe, Maybe, Maybe, Maybe.*

Article 13. Donna Gaines

1. To whom was the music of the girl groups directed? What role did the girl groups play for this audience?

2. Why might the music of the girl groups be described as "Producer's Rock"?

3. How is the girl groups' story typical of the role of women in rock, and in society in general?

4. Why was the rebel boy so appealing to girls at this time?

5. Comment on the author's assertion that girl groups' music was empowering to women, despite the fact that their music was written, produced, and marketed by men.

6. Were the girl groups a positive development for women?

7. Comment on the writing style. Why does the author begin with what might be described as filthy language?

8. Write a short essay on "Women in Rock: 1950–1963." (Note that you'll have to do some research in the library.)

Introduction

Sexism killed her. Everybody wanted this sexy chick who sang really sexy and had a lot of energy . . . and people kept saying one of the things about her was that she was just 'one of the guys' . . . that's a real sexist bullshit trip, 'cause that was fuckin' her head around. Smart, y'know? But she got fucked around.

(Country Joe McDonald, who was romantically involved with
Janis Joplin for a short time in San Francisco, talking to
Deborah Landau in *Janis Joplin: Her Life and Times*)

I know it's a sexist thing to say, but women aren't as good at making music as men—like they're not as good as men at football. A girl in a dress with a guitar looks weird. Like a dog riding a bicycle. Very odd. Hard to get past it. It's okay on the radio, because you can't see them. Chrissie Hynde is an exception. Very few of them are exceptions. And if they don't have a guitar, they become the dumb girl in front of the band. I'm not a great fan of girls in pop.

(Julie Burchill, journalist and author, in response to a request to be
interviewed for *Never Mind the Bollocks*, London, 2 May 1994)

I don't think about myself as being specifically a woman as far as music goes . . . My vagina doesn't come into my guitar playing or singing . . . It makes me inarticulate and angry when I have to discuss my job in terms of my gender . . . I want to get to the point where women aren't treated like . . . giraffes. It shouldn't even be interesting at this point that I'm female and I do this. It shouldn't even be a point of contention. But it is. In a way, it undermines everything Chrissie Hynde and Patti Smith did, because it isn't any easier for us.

(Tanya Donelly, singer-songwriter-guitarist with Belly, during
an interview for *Never Mind the Bollocks*, Boston, 10 April 1994)

The future of rock belongs to women.

(Kurt Cobain, a few months before his suicide in April 1994)

If Bono Had Been a Woman, What Would Have Happened to U2?

Think of how many female musicians fit the description of 'rampant sex god with a huge ego' (a term U2's guitarist The Edge once jokily used to describe Bono) and, chances are, Madonna is the only one who will spring to mind.

Being a rampant sex god with a huge ego and a habit of crotch-grabbing has been the key to success for countless generations of male musicians, but taking the cock out of rock doesn't emasculate it. Cock-free rock has as much balls as cock rock, it can be as sexual and as sleazy. Witness Janis Joplin in the sixties, Deborah Harry in the seventies, Madonna in the eighties or Courtney Love in the nineties.

Women have always influenced rock as the passive recipients of pop 'lurve' in lyrics—the Beatles went for simple but effective titles such as 'From Me To You' and 'I Want To Hold Your Hand'; the Rolling Stones were more sexually explicit, with singles like 'Lets Spend the Night Together'. It would, however, be a mistake to think that women performing in rock is a *new* phenomenon, although the mass media tends to treat them as such each time a new batch comes of age.

Most of the women in this book arrived in the 1990s but all of them have been empowered, to varying degrees, by the enduring legacy of punk. From Courtney Love to Tanya Donelly, Huggy Bear to Echobelly, Björk to Liz Phair, punk has been the most pervasive influence, on both music and attitude. Some of the role models are obvious—Patti Smith, Deborah Harry and Chrissie Hynde—others less so—The Slits, The Raincoats, Sonic Youth's Kim Gordon.

Pre-punk, women had a much more defined and confined role in pop music. In the early 1960s, the so-called 'girl group sound' exploded in America—the Shangri-Las, the Ronettes, the Shirelles (the first all-female group to top the American charts with 'Will You Love Me Tomorrow', in 1961) and, of course, the Supremes, who had twelve number one records in America. With their love lost, love longed for, love left behind lyrics, these teenage girl groups were, on the face of it, successful But behind them were male songwriters, managers and Svengalis who shaped and engineered their careers and who dropped them as soon as they passed their sell-by date.

In the mid-1960s, 'girl singers' began to appear in the UK: Marianne Faithfull, Dusty Springfield, Sandie Shaw, Lulu, Cilla Black. They enjoyed more independence and longevity than most of their predecessors, but they still had the male business establishment behind them. It was, by way of example, the Rolling Stones' manager Andrew Loog Oldham who gave Marianne Faithfull her first record contract and who co-wrote her first single, 'As Tears Go By', with Mick Jagger and Keith Richards. He has been quoted as saying: 'I saw an angel with big tits and signed her.'

By the end of the 1960s and into the 1970s, singer-songwriters like Joni Mitchell, Janis Joplin and Carly Simon were looking to their own lyric-writing skills. Unfortunately, this didn't mean they weren't manipulated. Joplin complained of journalists quizzing her more on her lifestyle than her blues singing, sarcastically asserting: 'Maybe my audiences can enjoy my music more if they think I'm destroying myself.' The contradictions of Joplin's life were encapsulated in her attempts to be 'one of the lads' and, simultaneously, a 'sexy chick'. Her short life in the music business remains one of the saddest to date. She died from a heroin overdose in 1970, aged 27. If Joplin was portrayed as the rock whore with a heart of gold, the altogether more 'sensitive' Joni Mitchell was incensed when her record company sold her as '99% virgin' in the advert for her 1968 debut album *Songs to a Seagull*.

If every generation of female musicians includes women who in some way act as martyrs for the next, Joplin and Mitchell's experiences weren't all in vain. Seven years after the '99% virgin' advert, Patti Smith had a female manager and appeared on the front of her debut album, *Horses*, looking like a tomboy in jeans, white T-shirt and tie. Smith arrived at a time when there was a drought of women rockers. As well as an unorthodox singer-songwriter, she was also a writer and poet with influences ranging from William Burroughs and Rimbaud to Sam Shepard.

In *Idle Worship* (1994), Chris Roberts's collection of stars' thoughts on being fans, Kristin Hersh empathises with and eulogises Patti Smith:

> She was a first. I saw her as so physical . . . I guess she was just walking around being a woman. She was so jumpy and screechy, and always going from confused/delicate to confused/screaming . . . If there is a parallel between us, maybe

it's that she was dismissed as 'crazy' in the man-world of rock . . . She made an incredible mark, with dignity. She's a landmark, all by herself.

Smith came out of the fledgling New York art rock scene in the mid 1970s and found herself immediately 'at home' in the new freedom offered by the decade's latest cultural phenomenon. Punk.

In 1976 punk happened in the UK. It was anti-hippie protest music fuelled by speed rather than marijuana. Its DIY ethos and anti-muso attitude allowed women a much-needed space to perform without fear of ridicule. Punk was about everyone starting from scratch and throwing away traditional rock clichés. It was lo-fi, chaotic, basic. It was exciting, unpredictable and anti-fashion.

Punk made female performers truly visible and gave them a unique forum for the first time. As Gillian G. Gaar affirms in *She's a Rebel: The History of Women in Rock & Roll* (1992): 'If feminism had inspired women to create their own opportunities, punk offered women a specific realm in which to create their own opportunities as musicians.' Using fanzines as a grassroots way of communicating, and developing small, independent labels to sign new acts, punk avoided relying on the mainstream music press and the anonymous suits running big, corporate record labels. It lasted barely two years (1976–78), but its impact on white urban teenagers was dramatic.

Poly Styrene, who fronted X-Ray Spex, presented the world with punk's first female, asexual, aggressive persona. The Slits—with Ari Up on vocals, Viv Albertine on guitar, Palmolive on drums and Tessa Pollitt on bass—made an amateurish, cacophonous sound that was, for many, the real spirit of punk. They ran into trouble with the cover of their first album, *Cut*, caking their bodies in mud and appearing naked except for loincloths. *They* said they were parodying the received images of women; for others they were simply pandering to the traditional marketing of female musicians. But, initially at least, punk operated in a hazily defined area where playing with these sorts of contradictions was part and parcel of the whole cultural dynamic. The Raincoats, who were joined by Palmolive when she left the Slits in

1978, also addressed the issue of gender and image, while making more conceptual music than many of their peers. (Two decades later they were cited as a prime influence by the likes of Kurt Cobain and Courtney Love.)

The only real punk band fronted by a woman to stay around for any length of time was Siouxsie and the Banshees. Siouxsie Sioux, like many women who joined punk bands, was a fan first—before getting up on stage and singing like a demented wild child, she was a devout Sex Pistols groupie. Siouxsie became a significant cult icon for female adolescents, responsible for launching a nation of lookalikes who dressed in black, stuck their hair up and out, painted black triangles round their eyes, didn't smile very often—and who later, at the start of the 1980s, denied being Goths.

If Siouxsie was the first punk rock woman to be widely cloned, Deborah (then Debbie) Harry was punk's first female pin-up. Her sexy image appealed to girls as well as boys; she was the first female musician that girls could admit to having a crush on. She exuded something previously associated only with male musicians: cool. Harry's band, Blondie, initially fused the chaos of punk with girl group melodies, and their 1978 album *Parallel Lines* became—along with the Sex Pistols' *Never Mind the Bollocks* (1977)—an album every self-respecting punk record collector had to own.

Born in Miami, Florida in 1945, Deborah Harry moved to New York 'to be a performer'. She was briefly in a band called Wind in the Willows and (infamously) a *Playboy* bunny waitress. She bleached her hair for the first time in 1959 and the look stuck. With Blondie, which she formed with sometime lover Chris Stein in 1974, Harry became Andy Warhol's favourite pop star and a tough, glamorous singer-songwriter—sassy, sexy and in control. Her barbed lyrics were sweetened with a saccharin smile. On 'Heart of Glass' she sang: 'Once had a love and it was a gas, soon turned out to be a pain in the ass.'

Yet, despite her hand in the band's songwriting ('One Way or Another', 'Call Me', 'Dreaming', amongst others), Harry remained a pin-up. The game she played was a dangerous one: flaunting her high cheekbones, slightly tarty image and traditional, up-front sex appeal. At times it appeared to the music business that she was little more than a package perfectly suited to the male fantasy factor. She certainly used her glamour to sell her product, but when her record company used her sexuality to encourage the fantasy factor, she decided it was time to regain control. The promotional poster for her debut single, 'Rip Her to Shreds', featured the provocative line: 'Wouldn't You Like to Rip Her To Shreds?' 'I was *furious* when I saw that fuckin' ad! I told them not to fuckin' put it out anymore—and they didn't,' she told Tony Parsons in a *New Musical Express* interview in the summer of 1978.

In an extensive profile of Deborah Harry in the August 1993 issue of Q, Tom Hibbert writes: 'She was The New Monroe, The Punk Garbo. Now there are 488 Rock Femmes. Madonna is one of them, Wendy James is another and it's all *her* fault. Debbie Harry changed the face of civilisation and popular culture and music and everything else as we know it.' Harry is a role model *extraordinaire*. She has influenced everyone from Madonna—'she (Madonna) mentioned I was important to her. That's very satisfying, but a check would be better'—to 1994's media-created, retro-punky New Wave Of New Wave. Justine Frischmann of Elastica told *SKY* magazine: '*Parallel Lines* was the first record I really got into. The thing that was so appealing about her look was that she was both soft and hard. Her look is part angel, part prostitute. It comes across in her singing, too.'

Like Harry, Chrissie Hynde is a true rock 'n' roll survivor (she has also been called a female Keith Richards). She was born in Ohio but was inspired by British punk and, like Harry, Hynde was a late developer. She was already in her late twenties when the Pretenders' self-titled debut album hit the top of the American album charts in 1980. Hynde's music and look was defined by a distinctly pre-punk aesthetic. And, like Harry, she had had to wait for punk to come along for her music to be taken seriously. In her chapter in this book, Veruca Salt's Nina Gordon talks about hearing the Pretenders for the first time as a teenager:

> I remember being completely floored. I heard that voice, saw the picture of Chrissie Hynde with her guitar, and I

learned that she had written all the songs . . . I had this moment of feeling really daunted and alienated—how did she know how to do that? But from then on there was an increased awareness that maybe this was something I could do one day.

While punk was happening in 1976, an arguably more dramatic development occurred. The appearance of the 12-inch single format had an impact that is still being felt today. While British punks were burning with boredom, this extended vinyl format was firing up the trans-atlantic disco scene, where everyone from Evelyn 'Champagne' King to the Bee Gees was taking advantage of the six- or seven-minute dance mix. A decade later, Madonna became the ultimate 1980s disco pop superstar—a female icon whose whole creative dynamic was forged in the New York disco scene.

Madonna Louise Veronica Ciccone's timing was immaculate. She was born in 1958 in Michigan (a year before Deborah Harry became a bottle blonde) and moved to New York aged 20, hoping to become a dancer. In 1983 the dancer-turned-singer crossed over from clubs to the mainstream with the funky pop single 'Holiday'. The following year 'Borderline' and 'Lucky Star' were both Top 10 hits in the States. The album, *Like a Virgin*, went on to sell over nine million copies. Madonna's success has been phenomenal. Besides being christened with the perfect first name and being an expert in the field of three-minute pop songs, Madonna is the ultimate female rock chameleon, teasing and seducing the world with a dozen different looks while ultimately being remembered for one persona—the vulnerable vamp with naked, blonde ambition.

Madonna's ascendancy coincided with the emergence of Music Television (MTV). By the mid-1980s MTV was redefining the marketing of music. It made *image* of central importance. In America, where cable television is as common as burger joints, MTV lulled a generation into thinking that the Look was as crucial as the song. In theory it was a great way of transmitting music from around the world—across the world. Soon, however, bands were giving in to the pressure to be 'MTV-friendly', to make expensive videos which seduced the eye, often at the expense of the ear. In MTV-land, a video is ultimately more important than the song it is promoting.

MTV means dressing up; contriving an image if the Look is lacking. For women, the predominant image that endures in the mainstream pop media is that of the 'rock chick' or the 'babe'. Female musicians are still made to feel they have to pay great attention to the traditional concept of 'beauty' or 'sexiness', the standards of which are defined by the male record industry and media. In this business, the likes of L7, or even Kim Gordon, are viewed as extremists, and indeed their music and attitude are informed by contempt for the marketing values and image-making ploys of the mainstream.

MTV arrived at the start of a decade during which, as Naomi Wolf writes in *The Beauty Myth* (1990): 'eating disorders rose exponentially and cosmetic surgery became the fastest growing medical specialty'. Wolf continues to argue that women in the 1990s may be 'worse off than their unliberated grandmothers' in terms of 'how they feel about themselves physically' and argues that 'We are in the midst of a violent backlash against feminism that uses images of female beauty as a political weapon against women's advancement.'

No one used video with such ease as Madonna. She told *The FACE* in 1990: 'I've always wanted to be a movie star. Even when I was a child, I behaved as if I were one.' From the early days, Madonna realised that you had to have something more than a good record to sell and it didn't matter if your voice wasn't great. She packaged her image and presented herself to the world. Following Deborah Harry's lead, but taking the concept further than any other female artist before her, Madonna sold herself almost exclusively in terms of her sexuality. She went from a slightly pudgy, dull blonde doing a dodgy dance routine to a streamlined, pumped-up platinum blonde control freak with pointed bras and balls aplenty. And she knew *exactly* what she wanted. As Helen Fielding wrote in the *Sunday Times* in 1992, she is 'the belligerent beauty, the sexy warrior, vulnerable yet confident in her exposure, ironic, laughing at herself, playing with her power'.

Today, academics debate Madonna's place in 1990s post-feminist feminism. One of her biggest champions, Camille Paglia, American 'academic and commentator on gender', gushed in 1992's *Sex, Art, and American Culture*:

> Playing with the outlaw personae of prostitute and dominatrix, Madonna has made a major contribution to the history of women today. She has rejoined and healed the split halves of women: Mary, the Blessed Virgin and holy mother, and Mary Magdalene, the harlot . . . Madonna is the true feminist . . . [she] has taught young women to be fully female and sexual while still exercising control over their lives.

• • • •

If, despite her contradictions, Madonna remains the most potent mainstream female role model of the 1990s, many of the women in this book drew their inspiration from more contemporary female—and male—sources. Kurt Cobain recognised the feminine in himself more than any other nineties male rock artist and was, for many of us, a more subversive role model than Camille Paglia could ever hope to be. Equally important for most of the female musicians in this book, he identified the nihilistic apathy of a generation when, in 1991, he wrote about the futility of life in 'Smells Like Teen Spirit' ('I'm worse at what I do best and for this gift I feel blessed, I found it hard, it was hard to find, oh well, whatever, nevermind').

When Cobain put a gun to his head in April 1994, he became the ultimate symbol of angst for today's disaffected twentynothings. Cobain's suicide was reported and pondered upon in the UK; in the US it not only created hysteria, but was also seen as an acknowledgement of the hopelessness that had infected a whole stratum of 'youth culture'. With a single bullet, Cobain defined a generation—making the extent of their alienation apparent in a way that even his most intense songs had not.

That generation championed grunge. And grunge empowered women in much the same way as punk had. As the Slits and the Raincoats had done in the late 1970s, American bands like Hole, L7 and Babes in Toyland got up on stage and created a defiant noise that said: fuck anyone who doesn't like it. Direct sexual confrontation became the norm. L7 are all-female speed metalheads with an ear for an anthemic pop song: they pulled their pants down while performing live on *The Word*, and shamelessly threw a used tampon into the audience at Reading Festival. Their song 'Fast & Frightening' paid tribute to someone with 'so much clit she don't need balls'.

For a brief moment at least, gender roles were reversed. Kurt Cobain reacted against the hegemony of the male rock image by trying on his wife Courtney Love's dresses, by clumsily applying her eyeliner and lipstick to soften his angular face and give it a sinister prettiness. Cobain was the neurotic boy outsider who tended to be quiet, unassuming, even passive, while Love, initially dismissed by the media as someone who should be 'seen and not heard', voiced her opinion at every opportunity. He played the introvert Angry Young Man to her confessional Angry Young Woman. Love challenges all the received wisdoms about women in rock by taking on the verbal (and occasionally physical) aggressive male role, and alternating it with the female tradition of confessing. She often finds herself in trouble for motor-mouthing about heroin (ab)use and bitching about fellow musicians.

Grunge in part substituted cock rock with frock rock. In Nirvana's wake, male American punk rock bands like the Afghan Whigs and the Lemonheads relinquished macho roles and were photographed on music and style magazine covers wearing dresses. Frock rock worked for male musicians; for women punk rockers image was more problematic. Courtney Love and Babes in Toyland frontwoman Kat Bjelland are great on/off friends who wear babydoll, lacy, ripped dresses; slashes of loud red lipstick; platinum hair with roots visible. Love describes her dress code as the 'Kinderwhore' look. It's child-woman, a fucked-up Lolita, innocence disturbed. It is a potent, on-the-edge image which toys with vulnerability and power. It hints, disturbingly, at a 'rape victim' look, although both women would insist that they are ultimately in control. Courtney and Kat's image is less about artifice than, say, Madonna's; they are wilfully expressing themselves by whatever means necessary. Their music —fast,

furious, emotional and full of frustration—says much more than this image provocation can.

• • • •

Although it is slowly changing, the music industry is still male dominated and the music press has some way to go in its championing of female musicians. *NME* may be proud of its handful of teenage grrrl journalists, but from the start of 1985 until the end of April 1994, less than 15 per cent of its weekly covers featured female musicians or even mixed-gender bands. Of its 95 issues up to and including August 1994, *Q* magazine has put 13 female musicians on its cover; of its 50 issues, the younger music magazine *Select* could only find three such covers. Two of those (Elastica's Justine Frischmann dressed as a guy with a cigar in her mouth and Björk) are from 1994.

It is, of course, difficult to tell how these statistics relate directly to the number of good female musicians around. But when women *are* given space, it still tends towards the tokenistic. The May 1994 issue of *Q* had three female musicians on its cover. Björk, Polly Harvey and Tori Amos looked demure in white outfits under the headline: 'Hips. Tits. Lips. Power.' (The slogan was one of the catchphrases of summer 1992, when you couldn't move at the English rock festivals for T-shirts advertising Silverfish's song). They seemed a bizarre combination: Björk as the quirky torch singer/dance diva with the Voice; Polly Harvey as a dark, publicity-shy curiosity who could be a Patti Smith for the nineties; Tori Amos as the daffy, kooky character with Kate Bush vocals. They have little in common musically; what linked them, for the purposes of the story, was not so much their bolshie independence as their feminine 'eccentricity'.

In the feature, Tori Amos says: 'We have tits. We have three holes. That's what we have in common.' True. But she was overlooking something as unmistakable as shared body bits; what really links female musicians is not the fact that they play the same instruments, make similar-sounding music or share a passion for certain bands. From Courtney Love to Kylie Minogue, they have shared the same experience. They are not men.

The fact is that gender will remain an issue as long as the music industry is dominated by men, and female musicians remain an exception to the rule. While the infrastructure of rock is essentially male, from A&R to producers, from record company executives to journalists, female musicians may be successful—but in a man's world and on a man's terms.

The reality is that the world of rock music intimidates women on the most basic levels and this has held true from generation to generation. Most female wannabe musicians are intimidated by the idea of even walking into a guitar shop, never mind sitting down and trying out the latest model surrounded by a bunch of music lads. Women are seen as being somehow estranged from their instruments—how can they hump their own gear around if they are physically inferior? And in the late 1960s, Karen Carpenter not only suffered from anorexia (the disease wasn't recognised for a long time because she was thought to be taking a 'healthy interest' in her image) but was prevented from taking her drums on the road because they hid her fragile form on stage.

What's so disquieting about rock is that it presents (and prides itself) upon its liberalism, its daring and its ability to be subversive. Yet its liberalism hides a deep-rooted conservatism. If rock clichés traditionally number sex and drugs, there's a third equally important image: the groupie. The pervading picture of women's role in rock is as groupie and muse. Women approach music in a different way to men; they are more interested in personalities and their interest in music often centres around being a fan and idolising male bands, while the boys bond and train-spot, believing that a precise knowledge of a band's or artist's history leads to an infinitely greater enjoyment of their product.

While female groupies have been elevated to mythic status, they are also a reality. More so than in any other artistic genre, boys who are sad, spotty and socially handicapped can get up on stage and become sex gods who are suddenly wanted for illicit sex. Pamela Des Barres came clean in her book *I'm with the Band: Confessions of a Groupie*: 'I wanted to express myself creatively. I didn't know what to do or how to do it The nearest thing was to be with the people who created the music.'

If a fundamental male fantasy is to be surrounded by screaming, adoring women, women don't tend to need their ego massaged in such a way. Compare Jimi Hendrix's take on groupiedom—'I only remember a city by its chicks'—to Janis Joplin's: 'On stage, I make love to 25,000 different people, then I go home alone.' Female musicians just don't get the same buzz from the idea of sexually conquering each member of their audience. In a feature on male groupies in the *Guardian* in December 1993, journalist Miranda Sawyer has a simple answer: 'Men make crap groupies.' She continues by suggesting that perhaps it's a fundamental difference between the sexes that is the problem: 'It's not that women don't get the offers, it's that when they do, they are the wrong kind for women.'

• • • •

Rock needs to be constantly challenged by women. It is essential that it doesn't ever become antiseptic, clinical and fake, and implode. With the 1990s hot-pot of sexual confusion, women are able to construct their own images in a way they couldn't before. Men are still in control of the music industry, but women are becoming more acceptable. Real progress will come only when women have power at all levels of the record industry; when Arista's MD Diane Graham is no longer in a minority; when more women are writing about music; when female musicians are no longer a cyclical phenomenon; and when Madonna doesn't have to fight for 'male' power and independence to be 'free' to establish herself in her field.

Article 14. Amy Raphael

1. How have women in rock generally been viewed?

2. When, in your opinion, did women first really find their own space in rock?

3. Name three women who were able to take full advantage of the revolution in women's roles in rock.

4. What is the role of women on MTV?

5. Madonna sold herself on MTV almost exclusively in terms of her sexuality. How then can she be a "true feminist," as Camille Paglia puts it?

6. How did grunge continue the legacy of punk?

7. In what ways is rock conservative?

Living to Tell: Madonna's Resurrection of the Fleshly

Susan McClary

A great deal of ink has been spilled in the debate over pop star Madonna's visual image and the narratives she has enacted for music video. Almost every response in the spectrum has been registered, ranging from unambiguous characterizations of her as "a porn queen in heat" or "the kind of woman who comes into your room at three a.m. and sucks your life out," to formulations that view her as a kind of organic feminist whose image "enables girls to see that the meanings of feminine sexuality *can* be in their control, *can* be made in their interests, and that their subjectivities are not necessarily totally determined by the dominant patriarchy."

What most reactions to Madonna share, however, is an automatic dismissal of her music as irrelevant. The scorn with which her ostensible artistic focus has been trivialized, treated as a conventional backdrop to her visual appearance, often is breathtaking. For example, John Fiske's complex and sympathetic discussion of the struggle over meaning surrounding Madonna begins, "Most critics have nothing good to say about her music, but they have a lot to say about her image." He then goes on to say a lot about her image, and he too has nothing whatsoever to say about the music. E. Ann Kaplan's detailed readings of Madonna's music videos likewise push the music to the side and treat the videos strictly through the techniques of film criticism.

This essay will concentrate on Madonna, the musician.* First, I will locate her within a history of gender relationships in the music world: I hope to demonstrate that Madonna has served as a lightning rod to make only slightly more perceptible the kinds of double binds always presented to a woman who attempts to enter Western music. Second, I will turn to her music and examine some of the ways she operates within a persistently repressive discourse to create liberatory musical images. Finally I will present a brief discussion of the music videos "Open Your Heart" and "Like a Prayer," in which I consider the interactions between musical and visual components.

Throughout this essay, I will be writing of Madonna in a way that assigns considerable credit and responsibility to her as a creator of texts. To be sure, the

*Editor's note: In fairness to the author, it should be noted that the technical, music-analytical portions of this essay have been cut.

products ascribed to Madonna are the result of complex collaborative processes involving the input of co-writers, co-producers, studio musicians, video directors, technicians, marketing specialists, and so forth. As is the case in most pop, there is no single originary genius for this music.

Yet the testimonies of co-workers and interviewers indicate that Madonna is very much in control of almost every dimension of her media persona and her career. Even though certain components of songs or videos are contributed by other artists, she has won and fiercely maintains the right to decide finally what will be released under her name. It may be that Madonna is best understood as head of a corporation that produces images of her self-representation, rather than as the spontaneous, "authentic" artist of rock mythology. But a puppet she's not. As she puts it:

> People have this idea that if you're sexual and beautiful and provocative, then there's nothing else you could possibly offer. People have *always* had that image about women. And while it might have seemed like I was behaving in a stereotypical way, at the same time, I was also masterminding it. I was in control of everything I was doing, and I think that when people realized that, it confused them.

I am stressing Madonna's agency in her own self representation in part because there is such a powerful tendency for her agency to be erased completely—for her to be seen as just a mindless doll fulfilling male fantasies of anonymous puppeteers. This particular strategy for dismissing Madonna has always seemed odd to me because the fantasies she enacts are not very successful at being male fantasies, if that is their objective: they often inspire discomfort and anxiety among men who wish to read her as a genuine "Boy Toy." And I am rather amused when men who are otherwise not conspicuously concerned with feminist issues attack Madonna for setting the cause of women back twenty years—especially because so many girls and women (some of them feminist theorists, including even Betty Friedan) perceive her music and videos as articulating a whole new set of possible feminine subject positions. Fur-

thermore, her spirited, self-confident statements in interviews (several of which are sprinkled liberally throughout this essay) tend to lend support to the interpretations of female fans.

Yet Madonna's agency is not hers alone: even if she wrote everything she performs all by herself, it would still be important to remember that her music and personae are produced within a variety of social discursive practices. Her style is assembled from the musics of many different genres, and her visual images draw upon the conventions of female representation that circulate in film, advertisements, and stage shows. Indeed, in order to be as effective as she unquestionably is, she has to speak intelligibly to the cultural experiences and perceptions of her audience. Her voices are credible precisely because they engage so provocatively with ongoing cultural conversations about gender, power, and pleasure.

Moreover, as will be demonstrated throughout this essay, Madonna's art itself repeatedly deconstructs the traditional notion of the unified subject with finite ego boundaries. Her pieces explore—sometimes playfully, sometimes seriously—various ways of constituting identities that refuse stability, that remain fluid, that resist definition. This tendency in her work has become increasingly pronounced: for instance, in her recent, controversial video "Express Yourself" (which borrows its imagery from Fritz Lang's *Metropolis*), she slips in and out of every subject position offered within the video's narrative context—including those of the cat and the tyrannical master of industry—refusing more than ever to deliver the security of a clear, unambiguous message or an "authentic" self.

Thus I do not want to suggest that she (of all artists!) is a solitary creator who ultimately determines fixed meanings for her pieces. But I will focus on how a woman artist can make a difference within discourse. To strip Madonna of all conscious intention in her work is to reduce her once again to a voiceless, powerless bimbo. In a world in which many people assert that she (along with most other women artists) can't have meant what one sees and hears because she isn't smart enough, claims of intentionality, agency, and authorship become extremely important strategically.

Although there are some notable exceptions, women have traditionally been barred from participating in Western music. The barriers that have prevented them from participation have occasionally been formal: in the seventeenth century there were even papal edicts proscribing women's musical education. More often, however, women are discouraged through more subtle means from considering themselves as potential musicians. As macho rock star David Lee Roth (rarely accused of being an ardent feminist) observes: "What if a little girl picked up a guitar and said 'I wanna be a rock star.' Nine times out of ten her parents would never allow her to do it. We don't have so many lead guitar women, not because women don't have the ability to play the instrument, but because they're kept locked up, taught to be something else. I don't appreciate that."

Women have, of course, been discouraged from writing or painting as well, and feminist scholars in literary and art history have already made the barriers hindering women in those areas familiar. But there are additional factors that still make female participation in music riskier than in either literature or the visual arts. First, the charismatic performance of one's music is often crucial to its promotion and transmission. Whether Liszt in his matinee-idol piano recitals, Elvis on "The Ed Sullivan Show," or the aforementioned David Lee Roth, the composer-performer often relies heavily on manipulating audience response through his enactments of sexual power and desire.

However, for a man to enact his sexuality is not the same as for a woman: throughout Western history, women musicians have usually been assumed to be publicly available, have had to fight hard against pressures to yield, or have accepted the granting of sexual favors as one of the prices of having a career. The seventeenth-century composer Barbara Strozzi—one of the very few women to compete successfully in elite music composition—may have been forced by her agent-pimp of a father to pose for a bare-breasted publicity portrait as part of his plan for launching her career. Women on the stage are viewed as sexual commodities regardless of their appearance or seriousness. Brahms pleaded with the aging Clara Schumann (pro-

vocatively dressed, to be sure, in widow's weeds) to leave off her immodest composition and concertizing. One of Madonna's principal accomplishments is that she brings this hypocrisy to the surface and problematizes it.

Second, musical discourse has been carefully guarded from female participation in part because of its ability to articulate patterns of desire. Music is an extremely powerful medium, all the more so because most listeners have little rational control over the way it influences them. The mind/body split that has plagued Western culture for centuries shows up most paradoxically in attitudes toward music: the most cerebral, nonmaterial of media is at the same time the medium most capable of engaging the body. This confusion over whether music belongs with mind or with body is intensified when the fundamental binary opposition of masculine/feminine is mapped onto it. To the very large extent that mind is defined as masculine and body as feminine in Western culture, music is always in danger of being perceived as a feminine (or effeminate) enterprise altogether. And one of the means of asserting masculine control over the medium is by denying the very possibility of participation by women. For how can an enterprise be feminine if actual women are excluded?

Women are not, of course, entirely absent from traditional music spectacle: women characters may even be highlighted as stars in operas. But opera, like the other genres of Western music, is an almost exclusively male domain in that men write both libretti and music, direct the stage action, and interpret the scores. Thus it is not surprising that operas tend to articulate and reinforce precisely the sexual politics just described. The proceedings are controlled by a discourse organized in accordance with masculine interests—a discourse that offers up the female as spectacle while guaranteeing that she will not step out of line. Sometimes desire is articulated by the male character while the passive, domesticated female simply acquiesces. In such instances, the potential violence of male domination is not necessarily in evidence: the piece seems to unfold in accordance with the "natural" (read: patriarchal) sexual hierarchy.

But a kind of desire-dread-purge mechanism prevails in operas in which the tables are turned and a passive male encounters a strong, sexually aggressive female character. In operas such as *Carmen*, *Lulu*, and *Salome*, the "victimized male" who has been aroused by the temptress finally must kill her in order to reinstate social order. Even in so-called absolute music (instrumental music in which there is no explicit extramusical or programmatic component), the themes conventionally designated as "feminine" must be domesticated or eradicated for the sake of narrative closure.

The ways in which fear of female sexuality and anxiety over the body are inscribed in the Western music tradition are obviously very relevant for the would-be (wannabe?) woman musician. First, women are located within the discourse in a position of both desire and dread—as that which must reveal that it is controlled by the male or which must be purged as intolerable. Many male attacks on Madonna unself-consciously locate their terror in the fact that she is not under masculine control. Like Carmen or Lulu, she invokes the body and feminine sexuality; but unlike them, she refuses to be framed by a structure that will push her back into submission or annihilation. Madonna interprets the problem as follows:

> I think for the most part men have always been the aggressors sexually. Through time immemorial they've always been in control. So I think sex is equated with power in a way, and that's scary in a way. It's scary for men that women would have that power, and I think it's scary for women to have that power—or to have that power and be sexy at the same time.

Second, the particular popular discourse within which Madonna works—that of dance—is the genre of music most closely associated with physical motion. The mind/body-masculine/feminine problem places dance decisively on the side of the "feminine" body rather than with the objective "masculine" intellect. It is for this reason that dance music in general usually is dismissed by music critics, even by "serious" rock critics. Recall the hysterical scorn heaped upon disco when it emerged, and re-

call also that disco was the music that underwrote the gay movement, black urban clubs, *Saturday Night Fever*'s images of working-class leisure, and other contexts that did not conform to the cherished ideal of (white, male, heterosexual, middle-class) rebel rock. Similar dismissals of dance music can be found throughout the critical history of Western "serious" music. To the extent that the appeal is to physicality rather than abstracted listening, dance music is often trivialized at the same time that its power to distract and arouse is regarded with anxiety.

Madonna works out of a discursive tradition that operates according to premises somewhat different from those of mainstream Western music. Her musical affiliations are with African-American music, with a culture that places great value on dance and physical engagement in music. It also is a culture that has always had prominent female participants: there are no white equivalents of Bessie Smith or Aretha Franklin—women who sing powerfully of both the spiritual and the erotic without the punitive, misogynist frame of European culture. In critiquing Madonna's music, Dave Marsh (usually a defender of Madonna) once wrote, "A white Deniece Williams we don't need." But perhaps that is precisely what we *do* need: a white woman musician who can create images of desire without the demand within the discourse itself that she be destroyed.

Madonna writes or co-writes most of her own material. Her first album was made up principally of her tunes. She surrendered some of the writing responsibility on *Like a Virgin* (interestingly, two of the songs that earned her so much notoriety—"Material Girl" and "Like a Virgin"—were written by men). But in her third album, *True Blue*, she is credited (along with her principal collaborators, Stephen Bray and Patrick Leonard) with co-production and with the co-writing of everything except "Papa Don't Preach." She co-wrote and co-produced (with Bray, Leonard, and Prince) all of the songs on her most recent album, *Like a Prayer*. It is quite rare for women singers to contribute so much to the composition of their materials, and it is almost unheard of for them to acquire the skills required for production. Indeed, very few performers of either sex attain sufficient prestige and power within the recording business to be able to demand that kind of artistic control.

Madonna's music is deceptively simple. On one level, it is very good dance music: inevitably compelling grooves, great energy. It is important to keep in mind that before she even presented her scandalous video images to the public, she had attracted a sizable following among the discerning participants of the black and gay disco scenes through her music alone. She remains one of the few white artists (along with George Michael) who regularly show up on the black charts.

Her music deliberately aims at a wide popular audience rather than at those who pride themselves on their elite aesthetic discrimination. Her enormous commercial success is often held against her, as evidence that she plays for the lowest common denominator—that she prostitutes her art (and, by extension, herself). Moreover, the fact that her music appeals to masses of young girls is usually taken as proof that the music has absolutely no substance, for females in our culture are generally thought to be incapable of understanding music on even a rudimentary level. But surely Madonna's power as a figure in cultural politics is linked to her ability to galvanize that particular audience—among others.

To create music within a male-defined domain is a treacherous task. As some women composers of so-called serious or experimental music are discovering, many of the forms and conventional procedures of presumably value-free music are saturated with hidden patriarchal narratives, images, agendas. The options available to a woman musician in rock music are especially constrictive, for this musical discourse is typically characterized by its phallic backbeat. It is possible to try to downplay that beat, to attempt to defuse its energy—but this strategy often results in music that sounds enervated or stereotypically "feminine." It is also possible to appropriate the phallic energy of rock and to demonstrate (as Chrissie Hynde, Joan Jett, and Lita Ford do so very well) that boys don't have any corner on that market. But that beat can always threaten to overwhelm: witness Janet Jackson's containment by producers Jimmy Jam and Terry Lewis in (ironically) her song "Control."

Madonna's means of negotiating for a voice in rock resemble very much the strategies of her visual constructions; that is, she evokes a whole range of conventional signifiers and then causes them to rub up against each other in ways that are open to a variety of divergent readings, many of them potentially empowering to girls and women. She offers musical structures that promise narrative closure, and at the same time she resists or subverts them. A traditional energy flow is managed—which is why to many ears the whole complex seems always already absorbed—but that flow is subtly redirected.

The most obvious of her strategies is irony: the irony of the little-girl voice in "Like a Virgin" or of fifties girl-group sentiment in "True Blue." Like her play with the signs of famous temptresses, bustiers, and pouts, her engagement with traditional musical signs of childish vulnerability projects her knowledge that this is what the patriarchy expects of her and also her awareness that this fantasy is ludicrous. Her unsupervised parody destroys a much-treasured male illusion: even as she sings "True blue, baby, I love you," she becomes a disconcerting figure—the woman who knows too much, who is not at all the blank virginal slate she pretends to present. But to her female audience, her impersonation of these musical types is often received with delight as a knowing wink, a gesture of empowerment.

Madonna's engagement with images of the past is not always to be understood as parody, however. Some of the historical figures she impersonates are victims of traditions in opera and popular culture that demand death as the price for sexuality. Principal among the victims she invokes are Carmen and Marilyn Monroe, both highly desired, sexual women who were simultaneously idolized and castigated, and finally sacrificed to patriarchal standards of behavior. It is in her explicit acknowledgment of the traditional fate of artistic women who dare be erotic and yet in her refusal to fall likewise a victim that Madonna becomes far more serious about what have been referred to as "sign crimes." If the strategy of appropriating and redefining conventional codes is the same in these more serious pieces as in the "True Blue" parody, the stakes are much, much higher.

Article 15. Susan McClary

1. Why has so much of the literature on Madonna concentrated on her image rather than her music?

2. Discuss the historical role of women in music. How might this history have shaped the reception of Madonna?

3. What are some of the issues concerning women in today's society and women in music that Madonna brings to the fore?

4. How do the strategies of Madonna's visual constructions work in her videos? Can you name examples in addition to those described by McClary?

5. How has the role of women in rock changed from the time of the girl groups described in Article 13 by Donna Gaines?

6. Has rock advanced or hindered the cause of feminism?

Sisters Take the Rap
... But Talk Back

Helen Kolawole

'Who you calling a bitch?', asked Queen Latifah in her single U.N.I.T.Y. For many women rap fans the answer was all too obvious—the entire black female population. Of course there are exceptions to the rule—mainly the offending rappers' mothers, girlfriends and sisters—but any other woman with a sexual history is fair game for 'bitch-bashing'.

Latifah posed this question to all guilty rappers in light of the intense misogyny that has become increasingly prevalent in the rap world, and, in particular, in gangsta rap. When Aretha Franklin called for a little *Respect* almost three decades ago, she could not have predicted her plea would still be so relevant today. From the now infamous Wrecks' n' Effects *Rumpshaker* video, where women in swimwear shook their butts for all they were worth, to the censored groin close-ups in Snoop Doggy Dogg's *What's My Name?*, many female fans of rap have been left wondering exactly why they are listening to a music form that so often degrades women.

In the mid 1990s gangsta rap has become one of the most popular music forms amongst young people. Its enormous popularity transcends divisions of class, race and gender. But if the music has become synonymous with a profound misogyny, its artists can also boast a huge female following attracted by its energy and sexuality.

Gangsta rap is a distinct form of rap that originated from the West Coast of America. It draws much of its visual imagery from the blaxploitation movies of the 1970s such as *Shaft* and *Superfly*. The settings may have been updated for the 1990s, but the general stereotypes remain. Men feature as gun-toting misogynists who reinforce the sexual myths and associations of criminality that continue to plague black men to this day.

The image of the black woman has also seen little change. Women's role in rap is largely to appear as 'video hoes', placed on the screen for the titillation of the male audience. Very often the misogyny and violence become intermingled and indistinguishable.

In so much as gangsta rap is political, its main concern seems to be the plight of the black man. Gangsta rap is very successful at amplifying the

141

nihilism felt by the black community, but fails to go much beyond that.

Ironically, when rap first appeared on the music scene, it was hailed, not only as an exciting new black music form, but as a vehicle for social comment. In very broad terms, rap continues to fulfil this role, but (at the risk of understatement) gangsta rap has never been concerned with political correctness.

In the early days of rap, groups such as Public Enemy complained of their lack of airplay on mainstream radio and on the music channel MTV. Public Enemy came from a style of rap which posed specific criticisms of American society. But gangsta rap, while it claims to document everyday existence as it is lived in the 'hood', is not so explicitly political. Rather, it places the aspirations of its protagonists within the consumerism and individualism imparted by its Southern California origins. Concerned with guns, drugs and women, rather than collective action or concepts of black community, gangsta rap has gained mass appeal as the music industry has been tripping over itself to accommodate the genre's new acts.

But gangsta rap has also become the focus of a rather different form of attention—moral panic. In the States, the war against the violence and misogyny of some gangsta rap has seen the alignment of some strange bedfellows. From former President George Bush to Jesse Jackson to President Clinton, it seems everyone has something to say on the subject. African-American academics and politicians have cited many reasons for the phenomenon. In the main, it is agreed that the problem lies with the deep sense of negativity that has engulfed the majority of African-American youth. However, there has been a backlash by the rappers, who have instinctively closed ranks and closed their ears to criticism. Some of them argue that anything which comes out from the ghetto is legitimate, simply because of its origins.

There is some support for this view within the black community. In particular, the criticism which rap attracts from women is seen by some as divisive within the broader context. Speaking to the American magazine *Vibe*, Ben Chavis—the former head of the National Association for the Advancement of Coloured People

(NAACP)—expressed these sentiments: 'What I want to say is that I think it's retardant to the African-American struggle for freedom when sisters and brothers battle against each other. Our problem is not gender. Our problem is racism.' Notwithstanding the latter, there are of course many black women who would challenge Mr Chavis's assertions. Black feminist writer bell hooks has noted the dilemma that gangsta rap further poses for black women. 'I'm drawn to the raw sexuality that is expressed in gangsta rap, even as I am turned off by the misogyny that surrounds that sexuality. How to get an articulation of a raw sexuality that is not misogynist is the unanswered space in rap.'

For other black women, the issues are perhaps more spiritual. Delores Tucker, Chairwoman of the National Political Congress for Black Women (NPCBW), believes the misogyny and violence contained in rap is 'destroying the souls of our sisters'. Speaking at an anti-violence conference held in Washington in 1994, Ms Tucker denounced those rappers who indulged in the denigration of women, arguing, 'The continued dehumanization and negative depiction of women subjects our young people to offensive images that destroy their spirits.'

These are criticisms shared across some of the major divides in American society. Both concerned parents representing white middle America, where rap has gained enormous popularity, and parents raising children in deprived black communities, are worried about some of the messages being delivered on 'Black America's CNN'. Then there is Calvin Butt, the righteous reverend from Harlem on a mission to make rap purposeful again, although some have questioned the effectiveness of an attempted steamrollering of the offending articles in the middle of Harlem's main streets.

The solutions offered by the US government and the music industry have included attempts at outright censorship and the inclusion of parental advisory stickers on record sleeves. Similar tactics are used against white rock artists who have also offended mainstream moral values in their depictions of women and the use of allegedly satanic themes. But, as a way of controlling the content of both black and white music, these methods have more often than not backfired, guaranteeing heightened publicity and increased sales for the offending artist.

When many of the major record labels have come under severe criticism from activists for promoting misogyny, they have responded with some curious arguments. One of the most common justifications put forward by the music industry is the freedom of expression argument, something Americans hold dear as a constitutional right. Anti-misogyny campaigners have found this argument difficult to challenge. Jumping on the political correctness bandwagon (just at a time when the rest of America was jumping off it), the record labels claim to be providing an outlet for oppressed minorities to vent their anger. No such form of redress seems to exist for women.

Rap has consistently provided the music industry with some of the biggest-selling artists in the early to mid 1990s. But even its financial self-interest has been tempered by some artists pushing at the boundaries of liberalism. A notable, or rather notorious, example of this was provided in 1992 by FU2 on the flip side of their single *Booming in ya jeep*. At first the guys indulge in a little light S & M, such as safety pins through the woman's nipple, which is apparently nobody's business but their own. But the song goes on from what for many might be nothing more than an against the grain sexual fantasy, to a familiar world in rap that is apparently inhabited solely by the 'can't get enough fuck me 'til it hurts black bitch'.

The song was subsequently withdrawn by MCA after women workers complained to the company's executives. Could this be regarded as a victory for women who oppose misogyny? Sceptics would be correct in suspecting ulterior motives. The decision came at the same time as Warner Bros. were getting corporate cold feet over the furore surrounding Ice T's *Cop Killer* single. After protests from the police, from Warner Bros. shareholders, and from across the American political spectrum, the single was withdrawn, with the rapper's consent.

From a first glance at sales figures, it would appear that female rap fans have no quarrel with the intense 'bitch-bashing' that features in much of the lyrical content of gangsta rap. A great deal of the criticism vented seems to come from those with access to the media; not usually young black women. Rather we hear from indignant and enraged politicians or those seasoned in the delivery of sound-bites, not the fans themselves. Whilst the criticisms from those such as Dolores Tucker are of course valid, they are hardly from a generation of black women who could be described as fans of the genre.

It is inevitable then that female rap fans will look to female rap acts to give them a voice in redressing the balance. But how far is this viable? In the main, female rappers have gone no further than respond to what is produced by the men. This is not always for want of trying, but this reflects the position of all women in the music industry, unless they possess immense selling power.

Potential and established female rap acts face so many restrictions, never being allowed to cross the threshold into full-blown feminism, as their sexuality always remains their major selling point. There are exceptions to the rule, but, in the main, a female rapper must be seen as conventionally attractive, and maintain an accepted degree of sex appeal, in order to avoid being branded a man-hater or lesbian, or both. She may also find it easier not to attack her male contemporaries, for fear of being ostracized by the rap world. For black women artists who are already marginalized in the entertainment world, such ostracism may be too great a sacrifice.

Salt'n'Pepa have been the most successful female rap act both in Britain and the USA. The group has gone through several revamps since they first formed, but one factor has remained constant: a continual play on their sexuality. On the surface they portray the image of strong independent women who are in control, but the extent to which this is the reality is questionable. Near enough all groups, regardless of their musical direction, are subject to the dictates of the image makers. Today the group are extremely sexy; they may occasionally rap about 'no good men', but their liberation has not extended to being able to appear on stage without showing considerable amounts of cleavage or being clad in tight-fitting lycra. The image is strong, but it is still designed to be acceptable to men, even if men are not the main purchasers of their records.

Queen Latifah is one of the very few female rappers to respond in a constructive manner against the misogynists. Yet her stance is ambivalent, as she also owns a management company called the Flavor Unit, which has among its clients a rapper called Apache. Apache has in the past been known to indulge in a bit of 'bitch-bashing' himself, leaving Latifah fans a little perplexed about her commitment to ridding the rap world of misogyny. Despite this, Latifah's stance has led to rumours about her sexuality. She has on several occasions stated that she is heterosexual, but her 'unsexy image', along with her views, appear to be too much for the male-dominated world of rap to consume, with consequences for her sales.

Her 1994 single U.N.I.T.Y was a forthright attack on the 'bitch-bashing' that goes on both at street level and in the rap world. At one point in the track Latifah criticizes fellow female rapper YoYo for subscribing to the 'gangsta bitch' image. But Latifah suffers from the same problem as all her female contemporaries, whatever their image. They are simply not taken seriously, either by men or women.

YoYo is the self-proclaimed original 'gangsta bitch'. A protegée of Ice Cube, it might be ill considered to expect anything more enlightening from a woman who produces singles entitled *The Girl's got a Gun* or acts as a female pimp on *Macktress*. But once again it would appear that, like Latifah, YoYo is grappling with her loyalties, as she has played a leading role in the formation of the Intelligent Black Women's Coalition.

The Lady of Rage is relatively new to the rap world and at the time of writing had not completed her first album. She is the first female rapper to be signed to the record label Deathrow, and her debut single *Afropuffs* did amazingly well for a female artist. Rage does not appear to be subscribing to the gangsta bitch image. She is forthright and sassy, but, in an interview with the music magazine *Touch*, was reluctant to come out against the misogyny of her fellow Deathrow artists. In fact she sought to justify it:

I choose not to use those words. But people ask, how can I be around people who do. They're not talking about the respectable women who are out there doing their thing and trying to make it. They state plain and clear . . . bitch, ho' . . . you have those people out there. People who try to take what you have, or try to pin some kind of rape case on you for the money or media attention. I'm not a bitch, so I ain't never taken it personally. And they have never called me a bitch because I have never given them reason to.

Being one of the boys seems to be a rudimentary requirement if a young woman wants to get her career started. Then even when she has made it, the world which she has penetrated remains so male-dominated that it is easier not to speak out. If the Lady of Rage gave a disappointing answer to a subject about which many female rap fans feel very strongly, now listen to the rapper Snoop Doggy Dogg's equally tired apologia given to a *Sunday Times* reporter. 'I don't diss women. I got a woman manager, my girlfriend and mother are women. I don't call them bitches. Bitches and hoes are girls who come up to me after the show and try to break me off when they don't even know me.' If you did not know any better you might think that Snoop, whose lyrics point to a hard, blunt-smoking brother who cares more about his mother than the 'hoes' and bitches who inhabit his records, had been coaching his fellow Deathrow colleague on how to give a standard reply to journalists who keep asking about misogyny.

So what do female rap fans make of it all? If a great many female fans have a broad sympathy for what can loosely be termed the women's movement, how do they reconcile their feminism with their love of music? The fact that the majority of these fans are young does not detract from the seriousness of the issues. All the young women I interviewed for this piece expressed dissatisfaction, to varying degrees, over the lyrical content of gangsta rap.

Marcia, seventeen, dedicated Snoop Doggy Dog fan

'I went to his concert because I love Snoop's music. He's different, his sound is totally unique, you know, that Southern drawl of his is so appealing. Well I don't know how to put this any other way, it may sound strange, but I tend to ignore what he says about women. Sure, I think calling women bitches is out of order, but you just can't escape it. I think, if anything, I enjoy the music. You see, gangsta rap has a particular sound that is that much different to what's been around before. When I first heard Snoop rapping on a Dr Dre track, it was like a totally new experience. I think that gangsta rap is appealing because it is so raw, it's straight from the streets. In a way I suppose that excuses them using those words, because that's what they have been brought up with. But at the same time they could still make an effort to educate those younger boys, who do try and copy a lot of what they do and say. At the concert, when everyone was singing along with the bitch ho' lyrics, I didn't join in. I wouldn't describe myself as an out and out feminist, but I do believe in women's rights, so something inside me just wouldn't allow me to join in.

'I can't say that I'm a big fan of female rap. I like some of MC Lyte's stuff, and Boss, but there's not enough of them around. Salt'n'Pepa are really mainstream and I don't think people my age take them too seriously, but they do come across as being in control. These women have babies, hold down successful careers and look really good. When girls rap they sometimes diss men, and that's okay, but they are also positive in many respects. I think that men tend to concentrate too much on the negative and constantly get away with it, but I'm not sure how having more female rappers is going to change that. The change needs to come from the guys themselves.

'If I think about it too much then I would have to stop listening to gangsta rap, because it isn't saying anything positive to me. But it's hard because I do love the *music*. Do you understand what I'm saying—it's the *music* that appeals to me, not the lyrics. Any one girl in their right mind could not listen to a Snoop track and tell me, "Yeah, he's saying something really positive." You just have to ignore what's being said and concentrate on what makes you move.'

Some rappers, having become aware of the lack of positive vibes aimed at the *sistas*, have tried to redress the balance by turning their venom on white women. Amid the growing array of such tracks commending the beauty of black women is *Cave Bitch* from Ice Cube's 1993 album, *Lethal Injection*. In it he scathingly refers to 'stringy haired women' with figures like a 'six o'clock'.

Sweet T, twenty-three, lady DJ

'So he's gone from calling black women bitches to white women, so what? What's so radical about that? I must admit, when I first heard that tune, it did bring a smile to my face, because a lot of black women have a lot of anger about that. But when I think about it, I have played that track loads of times and I have seen black guys who date white girls nodding their head to it, and white girls dancing to it. How do you explain that? It's all crazy.

'A lot of girls have said this to me in the past, and asked, "How can you play this music?" Once, when I played *Cave Bitch* at a party, one girl came up to me and said, although she objected to inter-racial dating, that she thought that was the most degrading thing she had ever heard. I said, stick around, there's more where that came from. She was the sensitive type I guess, but she had a point.

'Believe me, I don't enjoy hearing guys rapping about sticking flashlights up women's vaginas, but my job is to play the music people want to hear, and that is what I do. I couldn't turn up at a party or a club and say, well this one and that one is not on my playlist for tonight. People would show me the door—a DJ has to play what is popular, and gangsta rap is popular at the moment.

'Personally, when I'm at home listening to music, I do "tut tut" at what is being said. I don't think the excuse that it is just a word is in the least bit acceptable, but I am in no position to do anything about it. It's like that ragga tune *Ride the Punanny* by Bagaworries, the lyrics are absolutely disgusting. Once I danced to it in a club and I actually felt disgusted with myself afterwards. But what can you do? The tune is kicking, I love the tune, but the lyrics . . .

'You see, rap has progressed, or some might say regressed, from what it was in the 1980s. When rap first started up it had a happy vibe. It was all about partying and stuff. Then gradually there came the Afrocentric stuff—and that was really positive and conscious while it lasted—and now, now we have gangsta rap. Peace and loving your Nubian brothers and sisters is tired shit now, it's all about reality. Guns, wilding, smoking blunts, how many homies you've lost, how much time you've done, that kind of thing.

'Women get a raw deal because they are in no position to answer back, and because rap has always been dominated by men, no matter what form of rap it is. I guess a part of it is that black men feel that they don't have to follow what white men do. So they can go on calling women bitches and stuff, because they are a law unto themselves. Why do you think so many black people, women and men alike, still believe Tyson is innocent, or don't care if OJ Simpson really did kill his wife? It's all about media conspiracies, but they never want to look at their own dirty laundry.

'It's hard for lady DJs. There are not that many doors open to us, and to get booked it's like a real achievement. So I could never exercise my principles to a club owner or whatever—I think they would just look at me like I was crazy or something. Long live the rapper who comes out and says enough is enough; but let's be realistic, no one is going to change a format that is so successful. I think it's a shame that guys feel that dissing women makes them even more manly. I'd like to see what would happen to Snoop if he called his mother a bitch.'

Some women rappers advocate hitting back in the same way. *Mai Sista Izza Bitch* is the title of a single by the female rapper Boss who directly addresses the use of the word 'bitch', and urges women to get even and do the 'doggin'. But how constructive is such an approach. Is this just an eye for an eye? And how difficult is it for women rappers to get the chance to talk back, let alone put across an alternative message?

Yemi, twenty-six, aspiring rapper

'I see no reason why women should not be allowed to retaliate to the crap that is produced by some of the male artists although I understand why they are very rarely given the opportunity to do so. You should see some of the reactions we have had from the A&R men. From their limited perspective it's bad enough that we're women, but when they hear our lyrics they almost choke on their coffees. It's always the same reaction. "You're good but I think you could do well to tone it down a bit." We used to say, "What's the it y'all don't like?" We would make them spell it out in plain English. I mean, could you ever imagine someone saying to Ice T: "Yep, yep, I think you've got real talent, but could you just go a little easy on the misogyny, you know how sensitive these women can be."

'We have rapped about doing things to men's private parts, but it has always been tongue in cheek, though there is a serious message to it. Have you heard of Bitches With Attitude? Well they are not really a rap group, but I can guarantee, if enlightened women were running the music industry, they would never have even got past reception, let alone be given a contract.

'Rap is essentially a boys world. Its images are there for young adolescent boys. It's like rock—the women there are providing titillation for the men, and those female rock artists who break through still have to look pretty and not diss the men too much. But just saying it's like rock does not excuse it—at the end of the day it is dangerous. It's telling young black men that they don't have to respect women. That they are nothing more than sex objects.

'As for all this "they ain't talking about me" bullshit—well I'm sorry, girlfriends, but it's reality time. I wish some of these young women could be flies on the wall when the men hang out. Maybe then they would realize that there is no distinction. For a lot of guys, "bitch" and "ho'" have become part of their vocabulary. They are words used to refer to women. It really is that simple.'

Josie, fifteen, waiting for inspiration

'Two Live Crew have got to be the worst for that, but I have never listened to them. I prefer the less hardcore stuff, or people who are saying something constructive. But if you go out, or you're in a friend's house and they're booming out the latest tune and it's saying something, then you're not going to appear lame and say "turn it off".

'My brother, who is fourteen, listens to all the gangsta rap tunes, and I hear him and his friends saying bitch this and bitch that. I just think they're immature, they are letting the music influence them. You know, some English boys act like they've just stepped off the plane from South Central LA or something.

'This is getting off the point a little, but I think it's relevant. When the film *Menace II Society* came out, I went to see it with some girlfriends, and we were amazed by the behaviour of the boys. Every time one of the characters said "bitch", it was like they loved it. I think they wanted to applaud. It's the same with rap. English boys know they can't go around calling girls bitches, because we will not stand for it. I can't understand how it's got to that stage in America.

'When I watch a rap video, and I see a whole load of girls dressed in bikinis, gyrating their hips around guys who have their faces in their crutches, I feel sick. It makes me angry, because I think I would like to be part of that scene. What I mean is, I like the music, but I sure as hell ain't gonna go around calling myself no gangsta bitch, or letting any man call me that.

'I think that record companies should take a stand and not allow the rappers to say these things. Sometimes when I hear it, it makes me ashamed to be black even. White people must look at us and laugh, but their kids are listening to it as well, I suppose. My mum sometimes walks in when my brother is watching MTV and she can't believe what she sees. In some ways it's the generation gap, but it's also a woman thing.

'A lot of my friends at school idolize Snoop, I don't know why; but they think I'm a bit weird, because I don't check for him that much. I tell them it's what he says that I don't agree with, but I guess it's hard to go against what your friends are listening to. Nearly every black kid in Britain listens to rap. If it isn't rap then it's ragga, and that can be just as bad at times. I can't say that I have ever aired my opinions to the boys at school because they would just shout me down straight away, they think they're so bad, as if they live the lives of black kids in America.

'If I controlled a music label, I would make it a policy that all my acts had to respect women. And of course I would go out there and find all those good female acts that had never been given a chance because of the sexism in the industry. I'm sure if girls started rapping about how nasty men are, then there would be an uproar. They would probably say, two wrongs don't make a right. But it would be a real eye opener to see their reaction. You have lady rappers like Boss, but what does she sing? "You gotta let a ho' be a ho'", and all that kind of thing. When I heard her last album, I thought she must be tripping or something, she was swearing more than the guys. The album was just full of bitch this and bitch that. Maybe she felt she had to outdo the guys or something.

'I like what I have heard from the Lady of Rage so far, but I'm disappointed by what she said in that interview. I think that deep down she knows it's wrong, but hey, Dr Dre signed her, didn't he, so what can she say? She's got to play the game. I am surprised though. When I heard *Afropuffs*, and she was talking about loosening up her bra straps, I thought, yeah—go there girl.'

There was a time, in rap's very early days, when a simple 'ho' consisted of something quite innocent—it was usually employed by a DJ to get a reaction from the crowd. He/she would shout 'ho', and the crowd would shout 'ho' back. But as the word took on a more lurid meaning, family acts such as MC Hammer were forced to drop these innocent rappisms, lest they be branded along with the rest.

The complacency of the music industry only serves to add weight to the argument that, just like the misogynist gangsta rappers, they don't give a fuck about producing positive role models for young black girls. If it sells in its millions, then that is justification enough for allowing artists to produce more and more of the same drivel. Female fans have little right of reply, apart from boycotting the records. But many of them do not want this because, as they say, they *love the music.*

As we have heard, the material produced by the female rappers cannot be relied upon to say anything more constructive than that of the men. Many of the female rappers appear to be in a quandary about the world in which they exist. Those behind the scenes will tell you that many of the female rappers actually do disapprove of the misogyny, but are tied by the constraints of the industry. For many female fans it seems ironic that, while the men are given a *carte blanche* to display every misogynist tendency they have, their female counterparts have to remain on the fence.

Some remain optimistic that things will change over time. Perhaps gangsta rap is just a musical phase that will peter out, only to be replaced by something else; but let us not forget that the 'bitch-bashing' has been around considerably longer than gangsta rap, and is not just the preserve of black music. Rock has an equally chequered past and present in this respect and to be fair to the rap world, not all hardcore acts employ misogyny in their lyrics, but—perversely and predictably enough—it is those who do who seem to gain the most attention, and for the present anyway, it is gangsta rap that predominates within the rap and even pop markets.

At least there is some resistance, but not all those involved are convinced of the benefits of outright censorship, nor can their differing agendas be reconciled. Meanwhile, female fans can only hope that more acts come along whose mainstay is not material derived totally from the sexual fantasies of adolescent boys. But they are not holding their breath.

Article 16. Helen Kolawole

1. Why do so many female fans enjoy gangsta rap, a music that degrades women?

2. Is there a way for rap to be sexual without being degrading to women?

3. Discuss "consumerism" in gangsta rap.

4. Should freedom of expression protect rampant misogyny?

5. Do today's female rap artists redress the balance? Do they combat sexism in rap? Or do they play the role assigned to them? Do they have a choice?

6. Is there a contradiction with female rappers who play strong independent women, yet project images made by and for men?

Appendix

Short Essay Questions

1. Write a short essay on the topic "The Role of Popular Music in My Life."

2. Choose and discuss a song or album that you feel best represents your life and the lives of your classmates.

3. Write a short essay critiquing two different reviews you read about the same band or album. What do you think are the elements a good review must have?

4. Write a short essay on "Women in Rock: 1950–1963." (Note that you'll probably have to do some research in the library.)

5. Write a short essay discussing who you think the first true rock star **or** rock artist was, and why.

6. How do **you** define the difference between "rock" and "pop"?

7. Write a short essay discussing the competing visions of the music industry outlined by Frith (Article 6) and Love (Article 7). Where, in your opinion, does the future lie?

8. Write a short essay discussing what you believe are the two most significant technological developments to influence rock/pop music.

9. Write a short essay explaining who, **besides** the Beatles and Bob Dylan, was/were the most influential artist(s) from the 60s, and why.

10. Write a short essay analyzing a song from any era (the music, **not** the lyrics) using the methods explored in class; or, if you prefer, create your own methods.

11. Many define rock in terms of its early (50s) and middle (60s) stages: as rebellion against pretension, against "high art." As John Rockwell (Article 2) has suggested, for them the very idea of art rock is "a cancer to be battled without quarter." Can or should rock aspire to the quality of art, or is raw primitivism its defining quality? You may refer to music or artists from any period of rock's history.

12. Choose an American city not discussed in class. Research and describe its role in rock's history.

13. Write a short essay on the topic "African Americans and the Early History of Rock."

14. Take two songs, one from the 60s and one from the last decade. Discuss how they reflect the political and social issues of their times.

15. In the year 2030, who do you think will be seen as the most influential artist of the 90s, and why?

16. Set up an interview with your parents. Ask them to bring a song that illustrated an important issue for their generation. What do they say about their song and the issue(s) it raised for them and their parents?

17. Discuss how "rebellion" differs for musicians and audiences in two different eras of rock's history. What is a rebel, anyway? And why is the rebel so appealing?

18. Write a short essay on censorship and rock, citing examples from two different decades.

19. Discuss image in contemporary hip hop. Must one "bling" in order to sing?

20. Bearing in mind that guilt is defined by *Webster's Dictionary* as "feelings of culpability especially for imagined offenses or from a sense of inadequacy," choose a song that represents for you a "guilty pleasure." Write a short essay defending the song.

21. Discuss a performer or band not covered in class that you think *should* have been, and make a case for their inclusion in future rock history courses.

Bibliography

Bibliography

1. Cohn, Nik. "Classic Rock." In *The Penguin Book of Rock & Roll Writing*. Edited by Clinton Heylin. London: Viking, 1992, pp. 37–41; 45–47.

2. Rockwell, John. "The Emergence of Art Rock." In *The Rolling Stone Illustrated History of Rock & Roll*. Edited by Anthony DeCurtis and James Henke with Holly George-Warren. New York: Random House, 1992, pp. 492–99.

3. Christgau, Robert. "James Brown's Great Expectations." In *Grown Up All Wrong: 75 Great Rock and Pop Artists from Vaudeville to Techno*. Cambridge, Mass.: Harvard University Press, 1998, pp. 126–31.

4. Bangs, Lester. "In Which Yet Another Pompous Blowhard Purports to Possess the True Meaning of Punk Rock." In *The Penguin Book of Rock & Roll Writing*. Edited by Clinton Heylin. London: Viking, 1992, pp. 103–6.

5. Garofalo, Reebee. "Punk versus Disco." In *Rockin' Out: Popular Music in the USA*. 2nd ed. Upper Saddle River, NJ: Prentice Hall, 2002, pp. 251–53.

6. Frith, Simon. "Introduction." In *Sound Effects: Youth, Leisure, and the Politics of Rock 'N' Roll*. New York: Pantheon, 1981, pp. 3–11.

7. Love, Courtney. "Courtney Love Does the Math." http://www.salon.com (June 14, 2000; accessed July 24, 2000).

8. Hamm, Charles. "Rock and the Facts of Life." In *Putting Popular Music in its Place*. Cambridge, UK: Cambridge University Press, 1995, pp. 41–54.

9. Martin, George. "19 January 1967: 'Well I just had to laugh . . .'" In *Summer of Love: The Making of Sgt. Pepper*. London: Pan, 1995, pp. 50–60.

10. Hicks, Michael. "The Fuzz." In *Sixties Rock: Garage, Psychedelic, and Other Satisfactions*. Urbana: University of Illinois Press, 1999, pp. 12–22.

11. Palmer, Robert. "Eight Miles High." In *Rock & Roll: An Unruly History*. New York: Harmony Books, 1995, pp. 157–73.

12. Walser, Robert. "Can I Play with Madness? Mysticism, Horror, and Postmodern Politics." In *Running with the Devil: Power, Gender, and Madness in Heavy Metal Music*. Hanover, NH: Wesleyan University Press, 1993, pp. 137–48; 150–51.

13. Gaines, Donna. "Girl Groups." In *Trouble Girls: The Rolling Stone Book of Women in Rock.* Edited by Barbara O'Dair. New York: Random House, 1997, pp. 103–15.

14. Raphael, Amy. "Introduction." In *Grrrls: Viva Rock Divas*. New York: St Martin's Press, 1996, pp. xv–xxxv.

15. McClary, Susan. "Living to Tell: Madonna's Resurrection of the Fleshly." In *Feminine Endings: Music, Gender, and Sexuality*. Minneapolis: University of Minnesota Press, 1991, pp. 148–55.

16. Kolawole, Helen. "Sisters Take the Rap . . . But Talk Back." In *Girls! Girls! Girls!* Edited by Sarah Cooper. New York: New York University Press, 1996, pp. 8–19.